LEONTYNE PRICE:
HIGHLIGHTS OF A PRIMA DONNA

LEONTYNE PRICE:

HIGHLIGHTS OF A PRIMA DONNA

HUGH LEE LYON

Authors Choice Press
New York Lincoln Shanghai

LEONTYNE PRICE
HIGHLIGHTS OF A PRIMA DONNA

Copyright © 1973, 2006 by Hugh Lee Lyon

All rights reserved. No part of this book may be used or reproduced by any means, graphic, electronic, or mechanical, including photocopying, recording, taping or by any information storage retrieval system without the written permission of the publisher except in the case of brief quotations embodied in critical articles and reviews.

Authors Choice Press
an imprint of iUniverse, Inc.

iUniverse books may be ordered through booksellers or by contacting:

iUniverse
2021 Pine Lake Road, Suite 100
Lincoln, NE 68512
www.iuniverse.com
1-800-Authors (1-800-288-4677)

Originally published by Vantage Press

FIRST EDITION

ISBN-13: 978-0-595-41699-8 (pbk)
ISBN-13: 978-0-595-87444-6 (cloth)
ISBN-10: 0-595-41699-3 (pbk)
ISBN-10: 0-595-87444-4 (cloth)

Printed in the United States of America

TO

JOSETTE SIMONE LYON

YOLANDE JUANITA LYON

AND

COLETTE THERESE LYON

One need not be a connoisseur of grand opera to appreciate the vocal talents of a LEONTYNE PRICE; nor is it necessary to understand the meaning of the languages from which her repertoire is selected. One needs only to lend an attentive ear.

PREFACE

When I first started to work at Time Incorporated in the City of New York in the late summer of 1962, I used to joke with Miss Genevieve C. Garrett, the librarian, and Miss Ellen Callahan, the cataloguer, about adding my future book on Leontyne Price to the collection of the Bureau of Editorial Reference. "It must be placed in the 'Locked Closet' for treasured books," I insisted. At that time I didn't have the faintest notion of ever having even an article published on Miss Price, although I had written papers on her in college.

For several years many persons had tried to encourage me to do some professional writing. However, it was my cousin, Mrs. Viola Redmond Sharpe in Rocky Mount, North Carolina, who tried to convince me that I was born to write a book on Leontyne Price. It took a lot of soul searching for me to tackle so ambitious a project. Since the late nineteen fifties I had collected every Price newspaper and magazine clipping I could get my hands on, although I had no intention of ever doing anything literary with them.

After continuous prodding from Viola, I met with Mr. Larry Dubois, a cover story writer with *Time, The Weekly Magazine*, and requested him to evaluate some of my material. Larry was very pleased with what he examined and insisted that I proceed to prepare it for publication. I, therefore, am most grateful to Viola and Larry for their confidence and encouragement during the early stages of this project. Mr. James Browning, Executive Secretary of the National Music Council of the United States, was also very helpful in advising me on style and research techniques.

I also wish to thank Mrs. Hattie V. J. McInnis, Leontyne's high school music teacher, for inviting me to stay in her home in Laurel, Mississippi, during the early months of my basic research. Along with Miss Flora Grace, Miss Price's third grade teacher, she aided me tremendously with life in Laurel during Leontyne's childhood and made arrangements for me to visit the singer's schools and the Saint Paul Methodist Church. I also listened to recordings of the Oak Park High School Choral Group featuring Leontyne as soloist under the directorship of Mrs. McInnis. I am appreciative for the warm hospitality of the principals, teachers and students of the public schools of Laurel, and for the information that some of them gave me.

Mr. J. W. West, Editor and Publisher of the *Laurel Leader-Call*, supplied me with many clippings about Miss Price's performances in several cities. He also permitted me to peruse the files of his newspaper. Mr. Owen L. Neatherly, Executive Secretary of the Chamber of Commerce of Laurel, was gracious in furnishing me with information about the early history and layout of his city.

I am indeed grateful to Mr. William Warfield for adding, as well as confirming, many details about Miss Price's early career and his marriage to her. Miss Betty Allen, Mr. Donald Barker, Miss Martha Flowers, Mr. Andrew Frierson, Miss Mary Robbs, Miss Katherine Van Buren and Miss Olevia Woodward were also most helpful in confirming information and supplying additional facts about Miss Price before she became popular.

Also deserving of thanks are Miss Carol Fox, General Manager of the Lyric Opera of Chicago, and the following members of her staff: Mr. Mel Kopp, Mr. Danny Newman, Miss Barbara Landa, Miss Janet Dalbey, Mr. Floyd Beach, Mr. G. Richard Ryan, Mr. John Peters and Miss Ardis Krainik. At the War Memorial Opera House in San Francisco, I was ably assisted by Mr. Julian Bagley, Mr. Cecil Thompson and the Staff of the Press Department. Mr. Lawrence A. Hill of the Public Relations Office of Howard

University in Washington, D. C., and Mrs. Dorothy L. Porter of Founders' Library arranged for me to use the files of the University's Moreland Room. Ms. Claudia Cassidy, Critic-at-Large, permitted me to read her files at the *Chicago Tribune.*

I want to thank the following persons for their gracious cooperation in conducting exhaustive interviews with me about Leontyne Price and in some cases about their own careers: Miss Martina Arroyo, Miss Grace Bumbry, Miss Billie Lynn Daniel (Frierson), Mr. Justino Diaz, Mr. Leonard De Paur, Miss Rosalind Elias, Mr. Henry Freeman, Mr. Larney Goodkind, Miss Reri Grist, Mr. Brent Hayes, Miss Constance Hope, Mr. Irving Hunter, Ms. Florence Page Kimball, Miss Juanita King, Mr. George Shirley, Miss Shirley Verrett and Mr. William Walker.

I wish to express gratitude to Mr. Bertrand Green and Mr. Harold Grimes for their generous contributions which made it possible for me to travel to complete my research. In addition, I am thankful to the staff members at Time Incorporated for their encouragement and assistance. I am especially grateful to Mr. Peter Draz and Mr. Benjamin Lightman for making my work schedule flexible which aided this project in becoming a reality.

Unfortunately, it is impossible to mention all persons who have shown continuous interest in this project and who have made significant contributions to its success. However, I want to express thanks to the following: Mr. Theodore Adelman, Mr. John Amury, Mr. Booker T. Arrington, Mr. Arthur Baker, Mrs. Beatrice Dupree Barnes, Mr. Ronald Brown, Mr. Albert Burems, Miss Veronica Butler, Mr. and Mrs. Benjamin Chapman, Ms. Harriet Chenault, Mr. and Mrs. Garmon Cooper, Mr. William Dovesmith, Mr. Gaylord L. Ellis, Mrs. Selma Ethridge, Mrs. Opal Lewis Fenwick, Mr. and Mrs. Ernest Few, Mrs. Sondra Funk, Mrs. Thérèse Genovese, Mr. Boris Goldovsky, Mr. Richard E. Grabe, Mr. Nathan Green, Mr. and Mrs. Albert Harris, Mrs. Alice Hirsten, Mr. and Mrs. Richard Hogg, Mr. Paul Hume, Mrs. Mary G. Hundley, Dr. Stanley Jackson, Mrs. Cynthia Johnson, Mr. and Mrs. James O. Langland, Mrs. June Layton, Mr. and Mrs. Michael C. Lyon, Mr. and Mrs. Carlo Medionne, Mr. and Mrs. Talmadge B. Portis, Mrs. Wilhelmina Richards, Mr. and Mrs. Jessie L. Roberson, Mr. Wilbert T. Roberson, Mr. and Mrs. Lawrence Sator, Mrs. Sherry Scott, Mrs. Patricia Sickles, Mr. Roland S. Springer, Mr. Earl Weber, Mr. and Mrs. Cleveland Williams, Mr. and Mrs. Leonidas Williams, Mrs. Mary Redmond Williams, and Mr. and Mrs. Russell Williams.

CONTENTS

Chapter		Page
I.	Early Life	15
II.	The College Years	35
III.	The Juilliard School of Music	49
IV.	*Porgy and Bess*	61
V.	American Operatic Debuts	73
VI.	Performing Abroad	86
VII.	Old Metropolitan Opera House	97
VIII.	Opera at Lincoln Center	111
IX.	Leontyne in Private Life	123
X.	Working with Leontyne Price	139
XI.	Discourse on Recordings	149
XII.	Leontyne in Concert	166
XIII.	Honors and Awards	182
Appendix A.	Leontyne Price: Principal Events (Listing)	211
Appendix B.	Leontyne Price: Opera Debuts (Listing)	213
Appendix C.	Leontyne Price: Discography (Listing)	215
Appendix D.	Leontyne Price: Honors and Membership (Listing)	217

LEONTYNE PRICE:

HIGHLIGHTS OF A PRIMA DONNA

CHAPTER I

EARLY LIFE

Approximately ten minutes before departure time the Price entourage arrived at the bus depot. It was in early September of 1944 and a torrid sun shone brightly from a lucid sky indicating that an Indian summer was almost inevitable. Mrs. Price, after giving a last-minute mother's advice to Leontine, embraced her daughter affectionately. Leontine turned to her Dad, planted a kiss on both his cheeks and made her final farewell.

George seemed more apprehensive about her leaving Laurel than his parents. He mounted the narrow steps and entered the segregated coach with his sister and placed her first new suitcase securely onto the overhead luggage compartment.

"Don't forget to write, Sis," he pleaded.

"I promise," she said sadly. "And you'd better answer!"

No sooner had George stepped back down to the platform, the bus started drifting slowly away from the station. Leontine curled up in a secluded spot by the window for her solo ride away from home. She pulled out a crisp white handkerchief and wiped her moistened eyes. Twisting around in her seat, she looked back for a last glimpse of her family, gently waving goodbye to them and to Laurel. The most exciting moment of the seventeen years of her life was punctuated with anxiety. The difficult task of leaving her parents and her brother was aggravated by a fear of what was waiting ahead. However, she knew that she could not remain in Laurel and carry out the plans she had carefully outlined for later life.

For Mr. and Mrs. Price this was a day of rejoicing. Both had struggled diligently through the depression years making all kinds of sacrifices so that their daughter and son could afford a college education. Like most Laurelites they had settled in the burgeoning milltown because its rapid development showed vivid signs of prosperity and offered new opportunities.

The flourishing town was born around a small primitive sawmill and railroad station in the heart of Mississippi's great belt of virgin pine timber. It was named for the flowering laurel shrubs which were so plentiful among the pines. Laurel is unique in comparison with most Southern communities because it dates only as far back as 1882. Its history does not include eventful traces of the antebellum South; nor does it have an old established society whose members can boastfully trace their ancestors back to the original settlers.

James Anthony Price was born in Enterprise, a tiny village located forty miles from Laurel. It was in the heart of an impoverished farming community. Primitive farmhouses, scattered throughout the hard red clay soil, were indicative of the poverty of the area. Unlike Laurel, it had suffered the pangs of the War Between the States and had never made a complete recovery. Many of its houses had been totally destroyed by fire. Slowly its dwindling population shifted to other regions in search of a better means of earning a livelihood.

Discontent with his lot, James left his birthplace shortly before the turn of the century. The adventurous young lad, born in the eighteen eighties about the same time Laurel was founded, had quit school in the ninth grade. He secured his first job as a laborer at Laurel's Eastman-Gardiner Lumber Company.

Katherine Baker was born in the northern sector of Mississippi in a village called Hernando less than twenty miles from Memphis, Tennessee. She had always dreamed of tending the sick and helping the disabled. To fulfill her desires, she enrolled in a nurse's training course at Rust College in Holly Springs. Her financial state did not permit her to complete her lifelong ambition.

An older sister had found employment as a maid in the home of the Wisners, one of the leading and most prosperous families of Laurel. Katherine, known as Kate to most of her friends, moved to Laurel in 1915 to live with her sister and her brother-in-law who worked and lived on the Wisner estate. Kate met James and the two were later married in a ceremony at the Wisner home.

Laurel was a white man's town and the color bar was as strong as in any other community of the United States. Negroes, making up almost a third of the population, occupied one section of the town and whites occupied the other. In ordinary conversation most whites referred to the blacks as the "niggers" without giving it a second thought. The two races were polite to one another when they met in the downtown stores or on the street. They would sometimes exchange polite greetings with a simple "howdy"; but socially, they were total strangers. Interracial gatherings were nonexistent in this deep-South town situated in the southeastern part of the "Magnolia State." Whites and blacks did not attend church together, send their children to the same schools, nor sit side by side in places of public accommodations such as theaters, restaurants and city buses.

James and Kate were both children of Methodist ministers and shared the same religious values. They had been brought up as God-fearing citizens and almost never missed church on Sunday. Their whole life was centered around the Saint Paul Methodist Church. The industrious young couple didn't depend on God alone to solve their problems.

James reported to work faithfully each day although he didn't earn much money. Kate, anxious to supplement the scanty earnings of her husband at the mill, started a profession of her own shortly after their marriage. Capitalizing on her few months of nurse's training, she began the practice of midwifery. She strove to build up a good reputation of delivering babies.

She collected a fee of ten dollars per child in Laurel and the surrounding rural communities. Sometimes her clients were unable to pay in cash, but Kate never turned them down. She gladly accepted a side of bacon or a barrel of peas as compensation for her services.

The Prices had not been married very long before they bought their own home; however, it was soon destroyed by fire. The thrifty young couple did not become discouraged by their misfortune. Within a short time they purchased another house. It was a one-story center hall framehouse located on South Fifth Avenue, an important thoroughfare running through Bonton. The new residence was more convenient than the first one because it was only a hundred feet from their church which was located across Jefferson Street.

Bonton, a black ghetto, was home for a large percent of the Negroes who were employed as unskilled laborers in the local mills. For the most part, their living conditions were inferior to those of their white counterparts. Most of the dwellings were sad-looking rundown framehouses and all the streets were unpaved. After heavy rainstorms, the ruts and water puddles made transportation almost unbearable for the mule-drawn wagons and the few existing automobiles. The denuded streets did not have tall green leafy shade trees to shield their shabby houses from the blazing Mississippi sun.

Kate Price was approximately twelve years younger than her husband. The untiring couple had been married nearly fourteen years before Kate showed any symptoms of pregnancy. They had almost abandoned hope of becoming proud, happy parents and began to make plans to adopt a child. Suddenly, Kate discovered that she was going to give birth to a child of her own. She and James were overjoyed. The pleasant thoughts of Kate becoming a mother for the first time brightened their lives. Their existence seemed to become more meaningful as they added preparations for the newborn to their regular daily activities.

The baby had been anticipated beforehand as a boy. A few months before the arrival date, a name had been selected for him. When Leon Peterson, a family friend from Washington, D.C., visited in the Price's home, he handed Kate a silver dollar and asked her a special favor. He scrawled his name on a door facing and made an earnest request: "If it's a boy, Kate, name him after me."

Kate, a member of the church choir, had a beautiful and clear soprano voice. She had never had any formal vocal training, but her voice soared above all the other members of her musical ensemble. She was singing hymns with the choir one Sunday morning when a sharp pang struck her warning that the moment of delivery was rapidly approaching. She and James had waited impatiently for the birth of their first son.

The firstborn finally arrived on Thursday, February 10, 1927. It was born in a front bedroom of their home. Even after waiting so many years the young couple was disappointed when Kate gave birth to a healthy girl instead of a son. In order to compensate for their disenchantment, they transformed the name that had been carefully selected from Leon to Leontine. Thus, their first child was called Mary Violet Leontine Price.

Shortly after Leontine's second birthday, a son was born into the Price household. The second child, named George, made the family complete. There wasn't too much money in the family, but both parents struggled hard and skillfully to make ends meet. They tried to insure that their children never lacked the things that other kids had. Although poor, they always had adequate food and sufficient clothing.

In the years before school Leontine and her little brother played in the long level backyard of their home. They often interrupted their games on the green grass to listen to their mother's sweet lyric soprano voice. As she pruned the rose bushes or hang out her weekly washing, she often hummed or sang church hymnals. The yard, speckled with a fig tree, a pomegranate and a pecan tree was an ideal setting.

Leontine got an early start into the music world when Mrs. Price went to church to sing with the choir. From the time she first began to sit up in her stroller, Mrs. Price took the child to the choir stand and placed her in a chair beside her own. Whether Leontine wanted to or not she had to sit there quietly and absorb the music while her mother belted out hymns during the Sunday service.

In September, 1930, when Leontine was three-and-a-half, her mother took her to Mrs. Hattie V. J. McInnis, a warmhearted music teacher in the Negro Oak Park Vocational High School. Mrs. McInnis accepted students for private piano lessons in her home.

Mrs. Price asked: "How young do you take them?"

"When they're four," said Mrs. McInnis.

Without mentioning her age, Leontine was immediately enrolled for instruction.

"I want you to give her everything," said Mrs. Price.

"That's a lot," responded Mrs. McInnis.

"She can get it, just give it to her," said Mrs. Price.

It wasn't until later that the new teacher found out that Leontine wouldn't be four until February. Every Saturday morning the teacher drove by the Price residence in her Cadillac and picked up Leontine for a half-hour lesson.

When Leontine first started her instruction, it was in the heart of the depression years and piano lessons were a luxury. Mrs. McInnis never turned her students away when they could not afford to keep up payments for their lessons. Sometimes Mrs. Price didn't have the ready cash and Mrs. McInnis always kept Leontine enrolled.

Leontine was so little when she started taking lessons that Mrs. McInnis had to lift her up on the piano stool. Once she wrinkled her cute little dress under her while she was being put on the stool and the little pupil wouldn't play a note until all the wrinkles had been brushed out.

Mrs. Price, with a deep insight and strong sensitivity,

began to take Leontine's music seriously. She had dreams of a great career for her daughter. Mr. Price wasn't too enthusiastic about the music lessons and didn't think they would amount to anything.

Leontine had shown signs of musical talent as early as age two. As she sat on her mother's lap one day, she listened to a local teacher sing a little song called "And the Little Brown Bear Said 'Bo'". Each time the teacher would sing, Leontine would bat her bright eyes and say "Bo a bo." The teacher was so impressed with the way the child responded that when she finished she told Mrs. Price: "You have an armful of music, there."

"Well, I have prayed for it and, if she wants music, I guarantee she'll get it," the proud mother answered.

Each year all of Mrs. McInnis' pupils were presented in a recital. The music teacher insisted that her students commit their selections to memory. Leontine was first presented when she was five years old. She played unusually well for a child of that age. Wearing a ruffled dress, her feet couldn't even touch the floor. Mr. Price, very much impressed with his little girl's presentation, sat there beaming with pride. He began to realize what his wife had been trying to convince him for a long time. After that, he wanted to help all he could although he didn't know very much about music.

Miss Maudie Jones was a third grade teacher at the Sandy Gavin Elementary School. Each morning she strolled briskly past the Price home on the way to her classroom. Shortly before Leontine was five, she used to follow Miss Jones down the street towards the school. One morning, the teacher asked Mrs. Price if she could take the child to school to spend the day with her. The mother gave her consent. After that Leontine would cry if she couldn't go to school every day. Each morning the little girl would be waiting on the porch. She would have her lunch in a bag which always included a shiny, bright red apple. Although Miss Jones did not teach the primer grade, she kept Leontine in her class anyway. The following February, Leontine turned five years old. She was then placed with her teacher, Mrs. Lela Dunlap.

Even after Leontine enrolled in school as a full-time pupil, she continued with her piano lessons. She made steady progress and on her fifth birthday, she came home from school and found a big surprise waiting for her in the living room. Her mother had traded in the family Victrola as a down payment to purchase an upright piano. The family had to make great sacrifices, but they managed to get it paid for on the installment plan.

There was never a problem getting Leontine to practice her piano assignments. Mrs. Price set up a regular practice schedule for her to follow and did not let anything or anybody interfere with them. If some of her friends called on her, Mrs. Price would say that her daughter would not be available until after she had finished practicing. Sometimes Mrs. Price would do her ironing out on the back porch and listen as her daughter played. At intervals the child would oftentimes call out: "How was that, Mother?"

"That was good but you can do better," Mrs. Price would answer.

Leontine did so well on the piano at such an early age that most people thought she was a child prodigy. Her mother had a strong presentiment that something unusual was going to happen to her because of her unusual ability. She became extremely protective, and wanted Leontine to have everything she needed. At times somebody in the house had to go without something in order for her to have a piano lesson. Mrs. Price was always concerned about her daughter having nice dresses to wear to school. If she didn't have the time to make them herself, she would buy them on credit in a local store.

There was always warmth and sweetness in the Price home. If problems came up, they were arranged in a very mature manner. If the parents ever argued, the children never heard them. Mr. Price always treated his wife with the greatest respect and always expressed the strength of his love. He was perhaps especially sensitive to her feelings because she was much younger than he.

On the opposite side of town stood the great stately mansions with their porticos, imposing colonades and carriage houses. There were pleasant paved streets lined with giant shady oak trees. This community was a marked contrast to the area in which the Prices resided. Up on the hill in what was called "the high house" lived Alexander Field Chisholm and his family. The Chisholms, one of the leading families of Laurel, occupied a large green house that was set back from the street by a wide lawn.

Elizabeth Wisner Chisholm was not only a woman of means, but a woman of culture and polish. Her father, Frank George Wisner, one of Laurel's most celebrated sawmill pioneers and lumber barons, had migrated from Clinton, Iowa, in 1897. He later owned the First National Bank, the first bank to be established in Laurel. Mr. Wisner was an orphan who had never gone to college but impressed upon his children the importance of education. He sent Elizabeth off to Smith College in Northampton, Massachusetts, where she earned a bachelor of arts degree in music.

Alexander Chisholm, a native of New York City, met Elizabeth while a student at Amherst College. After graduation, he married her in 1925 and the young couple settled permanently in Laurel where Alexander became President and later Chairman of the Board of the bank his father-in-law had founded. In addition to becoming a successful banker, he acquired extensive oil interests.

Although residents of the same town, the Chisholms and the Prices lived in two different world. The two families were brought together by Everline Greer, the aunt of the Price children. Very often Leontine and her brother would wander over to the Chisholm house to see Mrs. Greer. "Big Auntie," as they called her, because of her excess weight, had started to work for the Wisners before 1910 and continued her services with the Chisholms. She was the downstairs maid and prepared the meals for them when the regular cook had a night off. She and her husband, who was employed as the yardman, occupied a house in the Chisholm backyard a short distance from the Chisholms' home.

Mrs. Chisholm had three daughters and sometimes when Leontine visited her aunt, she would play with them under the watchful eye of "Big Auntie." Very early, Mrs. Chisholm, herself a pianist, observed that Leontine was a very bright little girl. She invited her to sing and dance for her family. Sometimes when the Chisholms had guests, Leontine was asked to come in to entertain them.

Like most brothers and sisters, Leontine and George had their little squabbles. But for the most part, they got along very well together. He had his little circle of friends and she had hers, but a closeness developed between them. Their early years were similar to those of children in any other small town. Leontine loved to play with dolls, ride her bicycle and play hop-scotch with her little girl friends. One of her biggest clashes with her brother was about her bike. After coaxing her into letting him take a ride, he disappeared with it and didn't return until it had been ruined. This caused a temporary friction between the two of them, but it was soon ironed out.

Leontine owned a gray and white bird dog named Queen. She loved her and liked to walk through the neighborhood with her pet accompanying her. George had a big German Shepherd whose name was Hitler. Mrs. Price was afraid of George's dog. Sometimes when she felt that he deserved a whipping, she was afraid to go near her son. If she had struck her son, she knew that Hitler would have gone tearing after her.

Mrs. Price wanted George to become a pianist like his sister, but she had far more difficulty making a musician out of him. After Leontine got her piano, George also enrolled for instruction with Mrs. McInnis. He was not at all interested and cared very little about it. A year later he had learned to play some duets with his sister, but refused to continue.

"Mom," he said one day, "I don't want to be a sissy."

George liked popular jazz. He was more concerned with the latest number on the Hit Parade than he was with classical music.

Leontine admired her brother tremendously. She always thought he was extremely more intelligent than she. But at times she found him to be a nuisance when she was practicing her music lessons. He would insist on playing his Nat King Cole records. This made her furious and she would take her complaints to her mother. Mrs. Price would come in and send him outside for some other activity such as baseball so that Leontine could continue with her practice without benng disturbed.

As a midwife, Mrs. Price had a special status in the community. People came to her with some problems that should have been cared for in the clinic.

"Go to the doctor," she advised them. "He won't hurt you."

Her clients had confidence in her and continued to stream to her for professional medical assistance.

Mrs. Price's profession helped to enable Leontine and George to enjoy more material things, but it sometimes created problems for them. The neighborhood children would often tease them when they saw their mother going out to perfom her duties of a midwife.

"You didn't come the right way; your mamma carries babies in her black bag," they would yell out.

Leontine and George often got into fights after continual harassment by the other kids.

Miss Flora Grace was Leontine's third grade teacher. She used to present annual programs in the school auditorium. Leontine learned dancing from her and also acrobatics. She became an excellent dancer and was the star performer on many of Miss Grace's programs.

While learning one of her stunts, Leontine had to balance herself on the knee of one of the little boys. She lost control and fell on her head. George, very excited, ran all the way home before his sister's arrival.

"Mama," he said, "Teen fell on her head."

Mrs. Price, unperturbed, looked at him and asked: "Is she dead?"

"No," her son answered.

"All right then," she said. And that was all she said about it.

Miss Grace, a disciplinarian, was very strict about her students following instructions and she always insisted that they appear on time for rehearsals as well as for the performances. Her programs were always one of the highlights of the school year. One season, in addition to dancing, Leontine coordinated acrobatic stunts with Rutha Lee Miller. Two swings were tied up on poles for the two little girls. Rutha Lee, two grades behind Leontine, was on one swing and Leontine was on the other. Gorgeously costumed, they kept their audience spellbound as they made their eyebrow-raising movements with precision.

Occasionally Leontine walked a half mile downtown to the shopping district with her mother or some of her friends. Most of the time she went downtown to the movies with Miss Flora Grace. There were three theatres in town: the Ritz, the Arabian and the Strand. Miss Grace and Leontine usually went everytime the film changed. They saw almost all the "shoot 'em ups," musicals and love films, but they never saw the horror movies. Leontine adored the musicals most of the time. She never wanted to miss the Shirley Temple films. When she returned home she would always give her mother a demonstration of what she had seen on the screen. She tried to dance just like Shirley Temple had done. She soon taught herself to tap dance by watching the Shirley Temple movies.

After Leontine had done so well on the piano, Mrs. McInnis had her come to her home for a second lesson on Wednesday afternoons. She also asked Mrs. Price to have her practice two hours per day. Leontine never complained when the number of her lessons was increased nor when her practice time was stepped up.

Like most young piano students, Leontine wanted to improvise on the piano, when she was with her girl friends. Mrs. McInnis, however, wanted her to master the basics of her music first. She realized that young pupils sometimes liked to play lighter music to entertain their friends. Nevertheless, she didn't want them to form this habit in the early stages of their music lessons. Mrs. Price cooperated wholeheartedly with Mrs. McInnis and gave Leontine specific instructions: "If you want to play something, let me know and I'll buy the sheet music."

Mrs. Price once had trouble with Leontine when she was about nine years old. She wanted the young girl to play "Blessed Assurance," but her daughter didn't want to.

"I can't play that," she kept saying. "I just can't."

She didn't know that her mother had a switch available. Mrs. Price approached her brusquely and gave her three painful lashes across the shoulder. Leontine played "Blessed Assurance" and played it beautifully. After that, her mother never again had any difficulty getting her to play the piano.

During the long depression years many children did not have a decent pair of shoes to wear. If they had two pairs, they were considered very fortunate. Mrs. Price always kept her children properly shod. Leontine had a shiney pair of patent leathers that were reserved for Sundays only. A plain pair of everyday shoes were used for school, the movies and for running errands. Some of the neighborhood children were less fortunate than the Price kids and had to walk barefoot along the dusty roads to and from the Sandy Gavin School. Mrs. Price gave her children specific instructions not to ever go barefoot. But Leontine would often disobey her mother and take off her shoes and stockings like the other children and tramp through the dirt and grass. However, she knew that her feet had better be in proper order before she got back in sight of the house.

Leontine reached her tenth birthday while in the fifth

grade at Sandy Gavin. Her outstanding qualities continued to unfold. She was already singled out by her teacher as a born leader. The attentive young pupil put all she had into everything she did. She was especially good in social studies and her papers were always very, very neat. Whenever she went to the blackboard, her work was equally neat. She liked to stand behind her teacher's desk at the board. The teacher always let her write on her favorite spot to the right of the teacher's desk platform.

George was also a good student at Sandy Gávin. However, he got off at a snail's pace in spelling. He had a lot of difficulty learning to spell the word "Wednesday." Mrs. Price, determined for him to learn it, tested him at home. Each time he would say "WEDDAY" she gave him ten licks and she said "if you don't spell it right you are going to get ten more." Again he came out with "WEDDAY." The anxious mother let him have it again with ten more licks. The third and fourth attempts were the same as the first two. George got a total of forthy lashes. After that it came out perfectly: "WEDNESDAY."

Mr. Price installed a homemade blackboard in the hall for his children to do their lessons. He always checked to see how they were doing. One evening when Leontine was doing her homework, her father observed that she was working a fraction by short division. He instructed her to do it by long division as well. "I don't have to do it that way," she told her Dad. Mr. Price insisted that she do it the way he had suggested. Leontine was very excited when she returned home from school the next day and reported to her father. Her teacher had requested that the whole class work the problem the same way that Leontine had done it the previous night. She was the only one in the class who knew how to do it.

Saint Paul was the first brick church to be built in Laurel for either black or white parishioners. The building was later covered with cement which was carved into block-shaped forms. Its beautiful green lawns with shrubbery bordering the edge of the church was an ideal spot for the traditional Easter Egg Hunts.

Each Sunday morning after an early breakfast, Leontine and George would get dressed and take off for Sunday School. George had to be forced out of the house because he didn't want to go. Leontine wasn't too keen on going herself, but she always gave the impression that she did.

By the time Leontine was ten or eleven she was playing the piano for the Sunday School. She later began to play for the regular church services. When the family returned home from church, they always had a big Sunday dinner. Mrs. Price, an excellent cook, always prepared a delicious meal. After dinner, George very often went for a ride on his bicycle while Leontine and Mrs. Price washed the dishes. In the afternoon, Leontine liked to stay at home to read or listen to the radio. Sunday evenings she played the piano for the church services again.

Leontine started to make money for herself by doing little piano jobs around town. She began to do soirée performances for the Chisholm family. She either sang or played the piano for them. When she performed at parties in the evening, her brother would accompany her home or the Chisholms would send her with a taxi driver they trusted.

Leontine became a local success at an early age and was often asked to sing for funerals and weddings. Someone would contact her saying, "Somebody's getting married," or "somebody died." She was paid a small fee for her services and she was proud to be earning her own spending change.

Whenever she performed, she always sang with deep feeling and sensitivity. On one occasion a group of mourners became very emotional over one of her performances at a funeral. She was asked to stop singing to keep from further upsetting the bereaved family. She didn't continue, but became extremely angry.

"That's the last funeral I'll do," she declared.

In the fall of 1937, Leontine entered the Oak Park

Vocational High School as a sixth grade student. Although segregated, it was one of the best high schools in the state of Mississippi. Having completed her studies as an "A student" at Sandy Gavin, she was already looked upon throughout her hometown as one of the students who was most likely to succeed.

Oak Park was chiefly a vocational school and courses in the arts were limited. One of the most popular courses for young girls was domestic science. However, Leontine had her sights set on making preparations for college. Mrs. Hattie V. J. McInnis had a very effective music program and taught her students "public school music." They learned all the fundamentals which included basic piano information, the make-up of the families of instruments, theory, harmony, scales and chords. Mrs. McInnis permitted each student to advance according to his individual ability. The "fast movers" were given additional material.

The Oak Park Choral Group, under the directorship of Mrs. McInnis, had established the coveted reputation of winning in district as well as state festivals throughout Mississippi. It was a high honor to be among the chosen few who sang with the group. Mrs. McInnis had strict auditions for the Choral Group and she wouldn't utter a word after each student performed for her. Later, she posted on the bulletin board the names of those students she had selected with care.

Mrs. McInnis got permission from the parents of the advanced piano students for them to be trained to accompany the Choral Group. She, therefore, very seldom had to play for the group herself. Leontine was selected to play for all the school concerts.

In addition to travelling to other cities, the Choral Group performed in local churches of Laurel. Persons of the ensemble whose church was the host would sing the leading roles.

Mrs. McInnis did not permit her Choral Group members to participate in the pep squad. She said that vocal students could not control their voices if they had to yell. "If you are going to holler," she said, "you can't sing. If you are going to sing, you can't holler."

Both Leontine and George sang with the Choral Group. Although Leontine had a wide range, she always sang first soprano. She was one of the most talented among her contemporaries and was the star performer. However, Mrs. McInnis worked with her in the same manner she did the others and, consequently, there was no apparent jealousy among the other singers. When Leontine erred, she was given the same degree of punishment as the others. Sometimes she wanted to chew gum or had a tendency to giggle. Whenever she was caught, she was chastized by her teacher.

One day George went home and reported to his mother that Leontine had been whipped by Mrs. McInnis. Mrs. Price warned her daughter emphatically; "If you get another whipping from your teacher, you are going to get three altogether. The one from the teacher, one from your father, and one from me." After that, there was no problem with Leontine.

Olevia Woodward was one of Leontine's best friends. She was in the Oak Park class of 1945. She also sang and travelled with the Choral Group. She attended parties and dances with Leontine. Sometimes the girls went to the local movie houses together. They always liked to go on Mondays and would munch on candy while watching films from the balcony. Isabelle Jones was also one of Leontine's movie companions and one of her closest girlfriends. Leontine loved the movies and particularly liked *Gone With the Wind* and *Grapes of Wrath*. She almost never stopped talking about them after she had seen them.

Most young girls started dating at age sixteen and were married by the time they reached eighteen. Mr. and Mrs. Price were extremely strict about Leontine having dates and did not permit her to run the streets like some of the other kids did. They were determined for their daughter to go through high school with honors and continue on to college even if it meant taking out a mortgage on their home.

Leontine, therefore, didn't do any heavy dating and very often stayed at home to cook for the family when her mother went out to deliver babies. Most of her girl friends didn't take the boys seriously either. Some of them would get a big thrill out of exchanging letters with the boys they admired at school. Mr. and Mrs. Price permitted Leontine to attend parties if they were certain no alcoholic beverages would be served. The parties always started early and did not last late. Usually there was a piano for music accompaniment at house parties. Groups of young teenagers got together to listen to the music or play parlor games. Leontine, an excellent dancer, sometimes went to a small club called the White Castle. She always had an amusing time in the presence of many of her friends who danced to the music of one of the local groups.

In 1943 Oak Park celebrated National Music week through bulletin posters made by music students and supervised by Mrs. McInnis. The posters not only covered the most famous of the black musicians in song and instrument, but carried a list of former Oak Park singers and pianists who had excelled in the music world. A special list was made with a choral honor role giving specific details about former chorus members who were serving in World War II.

Leontine Price, the most advanced of the piano students, was accorded two chapel hours. She played selections of her own choice for the entertainment of the student body. Enthusiastically applauded by her listeners, she received several "curtain calls."

On December 17 of the same year, she was presented in her first recital by Mrs. Hattie V. J. McInnis. Among the invited guests who assembled in the Sandy Gavin School auditorium to hear the concert was Mrs. Elizabeth Chisholm. Olevia Woodward and some of the other members of the Choral Group served as ushers for the occasion.

The gifted young recitalist sang as well as played the piano. Some of the piano selections of her program were the "Prelude in C Sharp Minor" by Rachmaninoff, "Minuet in G" by I. J. Pederewski and "Concerto in B Flat Minor" by Tschaikowsky.

Her listeners also heard her interpretation of popular songs which included the "Bugle Boy Boogie," "The Man I Love" and "White Christmas." A special delight of the evening was her own arrangement of "Deep River."

Her piano renditions, as well as her vocal style and delivery showed obvious signs of promise. With a unique strut, Leontine appeared several times to take bows at the insistence of her audience.

Leontine's high school days encompassed more than music. She was well liked by her teachers as well as her classmates. She seemed to specialize in everything and did well academically. If her grades were not pleasing to her, she became very upset.

As a drum majorette, Leontine used to go on trips with the football team to Hattiesburg and Meridian. Some of the students constructed a fence around the Oak Park football field. It was made of wire covered with sacks. They called it the "Sack Bowl." At half time Leontine would be seen walking around the field on her hands.

During her senior year in high school, she was determined to win the title of Miss Oak Park. The winner, by tradition, is the girl who raises the most money for school projects. Going from door to door, she asked her friends for their financial support. She touched Mr. Chisholm when she went to see him and sang his favorite song, "Mah Lindy Lou." In her final count she discovered that she had collected thirty-five dollars of the ninety dollars total raised by the entire class. Leontine indisputably earned the title of "Miss Oak Park" that year.

Graduating *cum laude* from high school, Leontine was second in her class. She was also presented with an award for outstanding ability in music. Mrs. McInnis was deeply concerned about Leontine's higher education and wrote a letter in her behalf to Mrs. Marie Young Ware at Wilberforce College in Ohio. She informed Mrs. Ware that she was sending her a student who was very good in music. Mrs. McInnis requested that she help her by scholarship or by giving her extra work. Mrs. Ware wrote back stating that she would keep her and do all she could to help. "I know if you say she is good, she is good," Mrs. Ware replied.

CHAPTER II

THE COLLEGE YEARS

The village of Wilberforce is a small community located four miles from Xenia, Ohio. It has a history of significant activities relating to the underground railroad of the pre-Civil War days. Wilberforce College,* an ideal center for concentrated study, had nothing in the area that would lure its students from their classrooms. Although the campus was not located in one of the principal cities of Ohio, the student body was compensated by a serene atmosphere that was conducive to higher education. Cincinnati, Columbus, Dayton, Springfield and Wilmington were located within a radius of sixty miles from the campus.

When Leontine Price entered the college, she was totally unaware of the full potential of the unique talent encased in her vocal cords. The main objective of the seventeen-year-old student was to get a degree, return home and teach music in a local school in order to help pay George's way through college.

Wilberforce, a predominantly Negro college, was a site of natural beauty. Its tree-covered campus was divided in half by a ravine. A mingling of every tree native to Ohio and the Middle West were clustered throughout the grounds giving a picturesque effect. Its ivy-covered buildings and sunken gardens lent to an atmosphere of calm and dignity.

Leontine's voice first attracted attention at Wilberforce

---

* Later changed to Central State College, and finally to Central State University.

during freshman orientation week. As the determined-looking student strolled gaily along one of the tree-lined walkways of the campus, she was suddenly stopped by a group of hazing upperclassmen. She was somewhat perplexed until one of them asked:

"What can you do?'

"I can sing," she responded sheepishly.

And sing she did! The students listened in amazement as she sang "Because." When she had finished, each one of them just stood there speechless. The quality of her voice took them so much by surprise that they left her alone and didn't bother her any more; nor did they approach any of the other members of the freshman class. When Leontine returned to her dormitory some of the girls laughed and talked about the incident. Later they jokingly told her that she had been unanimously elected to represent them anytime a freshman was asked to do anything.

The ambitious young student had been offered two scholarships to college. Her Dad didn't want her to go to a southern school although both were located very near her home. She readily accepted a full music scholarship to Wilberforce which included tuition and fees, but did not cover the cost of room and board.

Catherine Van Buren was her first formal voice teacher. Leontine went to her twice a week for private lessons. The young instructor was absolutely delighted with her new pupil because she was so full of enthusiasm, very intelligent and quick to learn.

Miss Van Buren readily observed that Leontine was a "fast mover" and was capable of going very far. Her facility to grasp new material was phenomenal. When she was assigned something new in song literature, Leontine would come back to her next lesson with it learned. It was most unusual for any voice student to grasp the material so quickly. Miss Van Buren soon learned that Leontine would need someone who could take her much further than she would be able to do.

In the beginning she did fundamental work, technique methods, breathing and the production end of it. When Leontine was given small songs that new students usually began with, they were not enough to occupy her between lessons. Her teacher, therefore, had to carry her much faster than she did her other students.

Miss Van Buren was one of the first persons at Wilberforce to encourage her to go into vocal training. The music lessons at the college were only a taste of what she really needed, and the teacher knew that she was not equipped to properly develop her vocal instrument. Leontine was grateful for her teacher's interest and encouragement and continued to push forward.

Unlike many students, Leontine did not forget her religious upbringing after she entered college. It gave her a sense of responsibility and a feeling of security. She wanted to nurture it knowing that she could count on it in later life when confronted with difficulties. She attended church services regularly each Sunday and began to sing with the choir.

One Sunday afternoon as Leontine walked leisurely across the campus grounds she encountered Dr. Charles H. Wesley, the distinguished-looking president of Wilberforce. Dr. Wesley had been deeply touched by a very moving choir session at the chapel. He had been so much impressed by Leontine's magnificent singing that he stopped her and inquired:

"Miss Price, what is your major?"

"Education and public school music," she responded with caution.

"You had better think of changing your major," he suggested, "and emphasize voice."

She could not make a quick decision. There were too many things to consider before changing her future plans because her family had limited financial resources. It would be almost impossible for her to continue with voice training after she had earned her degree. Furthermore, a teaching profession was far more secure than a career in vocal music.

Leontine, an open hearted and generous young student, had made many friends shortly after her arrival at school. She soon became very attached to Betty Allen. Betty was not a voice major but she liked to sing for the fun of it. She had a very small, squeaky soprano voice. One of her big arias was the "Miserere" from *Il Trovatore*.

Betty, a pre-medical student, didn't think there was anything extraordinary about singing. Her godfather, himself a doctor, was on the Board of Regents at Wilberforce. He said to Betty: "You'll never make it as a doctor. Here you are with no mother, no father, no money; it's bad enough for women in medical school who have families with money. It's hard enough for men."

Following the advice of her godfather, she changed her major. She had done well in German in high school, and decided to major in it in college. Her facility for it was so good that she was permitted to teach a first-year German class at Wilberforce.

Leontine was one of her students. She loathed German and often whined to Betty in her southern drawl: "I can't stand that language." She liked French very much, however, and she excelled in it. After her French classes, she changed the spelling of her name from Leontine to Leontyne.

Although Leontyne had sung as the lead soprano with the Oak Park High School Choral Group, she began to sing alto with the choir when she arrived at Wilberforce. A well-known pianist who taught in one of the Eastern schools went to Wilberforce to give both a recital and a student lecture. Some of the music students auditioned to sing for him. He was very strict about everything. He picked all the students apart about their language and he found everybody's French atrocious. After Leontyne had sung one aria for him, he told her she was not a mezzo-soprano. He then wanted to hear her sing something written for the soprano voice so as to see how high she could go. He kept taking her up the piano and she went higher and higher without any difficulty or strain. Afterwards, she sang one of Micheli's arias which was written for a high pitched voice. He was very pleased and told her: "You have been using partials of the voice."

At that point Leontyne was totally convinced that she had a bigger vocal instrument than she had realized.

Very often Leontyne received boxes of clothing, food and other items from Laurel. Most of them came from her mother and Mrs. Chisholm. Betty Allen, an orphan, had been in a series of foster homes and therefore didn't receive boxes as Leontyne did. Whenever Leontyne got a package, she always shared the contents with Betty. Mrs. Price always sent boxes containing some of her delicious cooking. Southern fried chicken was one of her specialities. Although she hadn't met Betty, each time she sent her daughter a package, Mrs. Price always included something for Betty. At Eastertime, she always sent jelly beans and a bunny which she purchased at Laurel's F. W. Woolworth.

Mrs. Price was noted for making delicious fruit cakes for Christmas. One year she wanted Betty to come with Leontyne to Laurel to spend the Christmas holidays. Betty had no home to go to. At that time the vicious, foul-mouthed Senator Theodore Bilbo was raving with racial hatred in Mississippi.

"As long as Bilbo is in Mississippi, I ain't going," Betty told Leontyne.

Instead of going to Laurel, Betty accepted the invitation of another girl friend and spent the holidays with her family.

Leontyne was absolutely deluged with clothing. Mrs. Chisholm used to buy things in batches from Nieman Marcus and would send them to Leontyne. Although they were of good quality, she didn't always select the most appropriate colors to complement her skin. Most of the time they were dull, drab colors. When Leontyne got something she couldn't use, she offered it to Betty. Once Mrs. Chisholm sent her a very dark brown skirt. It was a loathsome color for Leontyne's complexion. She ran with it to Betty saying: "I can't wear this!"

As most of the girls at Wilberforce, Leontyne did not wear facial make-up. She had the most beautiful skin texture, but she didn't put anything on her face to make her look more attractive. Wilberforce was noted for its beautiful girls. However, most of them didn't groom themselves to their best advantage. Nobody had ever said to them: "This is what you do to make the most of your features."

Betty had always lived with a bunch of old ladies. Everybody's skirts were above their knees, but hers were mid-calf. Leontyne, measuring about five feet four inches tall and weighing a slight 125 pounds, was a very simple and plain-looking girl. Although very well liked by all the students, there was nothing spectacular about her except her voice. She was an average dresser who always looked fresh and neat. Very often she wore skirts and sweaters of different shades of gray which was one of her favorite colors.

When Leontyne went to Wilberfore she could play the piano very well. At times she was asked to accompany at school functions. She also could sight read. She willingly helped those students who were less gifted musically than herself. The students had a tremendous respect for her ability. Sometimes she was very temperamental and hard to get along with. However, she was especially kind and pleasant to individuals she really liked.

Mrs. Isabelle Askew was the directress of the choir. Very often she would get in her old Studebaker automobile and go steaming off somewhere. When she returned she had some old fashioned ideas that some of the students didn't find too correct. She was known to be very strict with most of her students, but she was more lenient with Leontyne. A marvelous student, Leontyne got very angry if things didn't go the way she thought they should. She would even walk out and refuse to sing her part. Miss Askew handled her with kid gloves to prevent this from recurring.

Clarence Henderson, known around the campus as Punchy, was a steadying force whenever Leontyne became evil and contrary. Punchy, a baritone, often sang duets with her. He could always communicate with her and could calm her down whenever she got upset.

Mrs. Marie Young Ware was one of the best instructors on the campus. She was never seen in gay colors. She always wore black stockings and very long dresses. She was a widow and all the students called her "Kiki." Mrs. Ware spoke immaculate French and she introduced the students to impressionism in French music. The students enjoyed her very much and spent lots of time at her house. Mrs. Ware pointed out just how precise everything had to be. She had perfect pitch and could pick out any one person among a large group of singers who was singing on the wrong note.

In addition to the Glee Club, Leontyne sang as the main soloist with the Wilberforce Singers, a select group of about sixteen male and female voices. The group was composed of the best vocal talent at the college. The young ladies usually wore colorful evening gowns and the young men were smartly attired in white dinner jackets and black tuxedo trousers. They performed on campus as well as travelled to various points in Ohio and the neighboring states to do concerts in order to raise money for the Wilberforce alumni.

The Wilberforce Singers went to many of the big cities including Chicago, Columbus, Dayton and Pittsburgh. One year, many of the ensemble were absolutely stunned when they arrived in Chicago and had the opportunity to meet Etta Moten, the famed singer. They found her to be such a grand, cultured lady and many of them were overwhelmed by her. Miss Moten was the first famous singer that many of them had met.

Donald Barker was one of the students who was inspired by Leontyne's cultured voice. He heard one of her performances when he entered Wilberforce in the fall of 1946. Leontyne, a junior, sang on a program that was designed to welcome the freshman class. Donald was deeply moved by Leontyne's touching interpretation of "Pace, Pace, mio dio" from Verdi's *La Forza del Destino.* "I have never heard such dulcet tones in my life," remarked the young student from Tulsa, Oklahoma. Donald, a tenor, was so impressed with Wilberforce's prime musical artist that he auditioned and became a member of the Wilberforce Singers.

One year at the Easter Oratorio, Leontyne replaced the tenor in "Seven Last Words of Christ." Donald Barker had been selected to sing the part but his voice lacked the necessary dramatic content. However, he did sing duet parts on Christmas programs with her in the *Messiah.* Leontyne easily handled the part at the Oratorio and came across beautifully to her audience.

College programs were usually held in Galloway Hall. It was an old building with a clock tower which seated about eight hundred persons. Leontyne sang there anytime she was asked and the student body turned out to hear her as though she were a national celebrity. The unassuming young singer drew standing-room-only audiences which usually ran as high as one thousand persons.

She sang spirituals as well as classical songs. The spirituals, sung in a subdued and reverent style, were usually accompanied by an operatic aria. Her most performed classical number was "Vissi d'Arte" from Verdi's *Tosca.* It was her masterpiece and she sang it beautifully everywhere she was invited.

The devout young student sang the "Lords Prayer" with reverence and beauty as no one else could. With an ethereal expression on her face, she often brought tears to the eyes of her listeners each time she sang it.

By the time she reached her sophomore year, Leontyne was well established as the principal soloist at school functions and had begun to participate in all the musical organizations on the campus. Her glorious voice drew attention anytime she sang and she always left her audience stunned.

She was the representative from Wilberforce at an intercollegiate music competition between delegates from eight Negro institutions held in Cincinnati. She won first place and was asked to return the following year as guest soloist.

Dr. Wesley thought she was a remarkable singer and continued to show keen interest in her career. He also had a good voice and loved to sing. In fact, one year he was one of the faculty members that teamed up with Leontyne to sing the *Messiah* at Christmas. Catherine Van Buren sang one of the soprano parts.

Dr. Wesley continued to make quite a stir over Leontyne's voice and never ceased to advise her astutely. He also constantly requested her to represent the school at special functions. She sang for such affairs as commencements and alumni breakfasts. Sometimes if the President was speaking out-of-town, Leontyne was asked to learn a new song within a short time. She always learned it quickly and sang it well.

As the top musical exhibit on campus she developed the delicate sensitivity of an artist. Her talent was well organized and everyone appreciated her voice. She took her singing very seriously and studied intensively everything she prepared. She did research on all her music so that the proper interpretation would come across to her audience.

If there were a program when visitors came on campus, it was always unanimously agreed that Leontyne would be included. The next question was:

"Now what else are we going to do?"

Her services were also requested when members of the board of trustees of Wilberforce convened or when officials came from other colleges. Appearing in what she called her "basic black dress," she always willingly agreed to sing.

One of Leontyne's favorite numbers for special occasions was "Homing." She had learned it back in Laurel. Her repertoire also included arias from the *Messiah* as well as operatic arias such as "Depuis le Jour" from *Louise* sung in English.

In 1947, Wilberforce divided into two separate colleges: one was run by the Methodist Church and other was controlled by the State of Ohio. Leontyne went over with the state side which had Dr. Wesley as its president. At that point, the Wilberforce Singers changed their name to the College Ensemble. When the students returned from summer vacation in the fall of 1947, there was a Wilberforce College which was run by the Methodist Church and the College of Education and Industrial Arts which was governed by the State.

She gained added recognition in Mississippi when she returned for summer vacations. In addition to singing on radio, she made public appearances in her hometown before civic clubs and as a guest soloist before Negro and white church congregations. One summer Mr. Boyd Campbell, a friend of the Chisholms, sponsored a concert for her in Jackson, the state capital. She sang for two different audiences the same evening. She thought that if the house were overflowing, she had to wait for the first group to leave and then sing the same program after the second one came in.

The frail young woman was not too popular among most of the students although respected for her singing ability. She would have had difficulty being selected as the most popular girl on campus. Although most students held her in awe because of her talent, she was not a loner. She was completely at home with the members of the Ensemble and devoted much of her leisure time to activities with them. She carried a heavy class schedule and didn't have too much time for entertainment.

Rosalee Simmons, one of her closest friends, was her roommate at Mitchell Hall during their senior year. The old hall, built in 1910, was a three-story colonial structure. It was overcrowded with ninety-five young women. The room that Leontyne shared with Rosalee had a double bunk, a single bed, a small work table and a dresser. It was decorated with drapes and matching bedcovers, sometimes had one or two other occupants. Leontyne and Rosalee, both members of the Delta Sigma Theta Sorority, collected figurine ducks which were symbols prized by their sorority.

At night both girls would kneel down beside their bed and pray silently. Some of the other students were surprised because Leontyne put so much of her ambitions and aspirations into her prayers. Before falling off to sleep, they often munched on saltine crackers between chats. When they had an eight o'clock class, they were up by six-thirty in the morning. Very often they took off to class without having breakfast.

Leontyne was never malicious or mean. Although she gave an appearance of shyness, she was outgoing and unaffected. She would tell her close friends everything. They always knew exactly how she felt. She was seldom interested in the fellows who liked her. During her freshman year, she had running crushes on different men although no dating went on between them. However, at times she would accept dates for parties or sorority dances and would sometimes stroll around the campus with some of the young men.

During her freshman year, Leontyne had an intense crush on one of the professors. He didn't know it but she was absolutely moonstruck over him. Her friends always knew the state of everything. She was either ecstatic or cast into despair. She became almost hysterical about him, but wouldn't say anything to him. There was nothing harmful about it and he didn't know what was going on. Leontyne almost never stopped talking about him. "He just smiled," she would tell her girl friends.

She struck up a close friendship with Jonas Waits, a World War II veteran who sang with the Ensemble. Although they had not met until he returned to the campus in 1946 after his military service, they soon found out that they had something in common. Jonas, a former resident of Jackson, was also a Mississippian. They met in a piano class and took many of their subjects together. Both loved their state tremendously and often talked about life back home.

They developed a warm friendship and called each other "Statey." Both were aware of the injustices in Mississippi for the Negro, but concluded that their individual childhoods had been pleasant and neither of them retained any bitterness.

This was Leontyne's first real taste of life outside the deep South. The college life was a complete contrast to her childhood back in Laurel. Students came to Wilberforce from all sections of the United States and Leontyne learned very quickly what others were like and how they lived. She respected their different ways of life but she didn't forget her own upbringing. Chiefly among her memories were the pleasant thoughts she always retained of her people back in Laurel. Very often her mind wandered back to the Saint Paul Methodist Church. Her family's whole life was centered around it. The church had been in poor condition as long as she could remember. It was cold in the winter and leaked badly each time it rained.

Although the condition of the church remained unchanged, Mrs. Kate Price was always present in the choir to ring out the words of one of her favorite hymns such as "Amazing Grace, how sweet it sounds, to save a wretch like me. I once was lost, but now I'm found, was blind but now I see." Leontyne, undoubtedly influenced by her devout mother, continued to offer her services at the chapel each Sunday morning throughout her college years.

When Leontyne reached her senior year she should have been practice teaching to qualify for an education degree. However, she was thinking more seriously about Juilliard and had abandoned all plans to return to Laurel as a teacher. Her decision to cast her lot on a professional singing career was definitive. As her years progressed at college she was singing more and playing the piano less.

It was arranged for Leontyne to audition for the Juilliard School of Music. She won a full scholarship to the internationally-reputed institution in New York City. However, the scholarship would cover only a small part of the total cost. Both Mr. and Mrs. Chisholm had become very enthusiastic about her voice. They went over to see Mr. and Mrs. Price to express their interest in their daughter. They did not feel that Leontyne should return home and teach in the Oak Park High School. As a teacher in the public school system, she would not have the opportunity to utilize her talent fully.

The Chisholms asked if they could help finance her advanced study at Juilliard. Leontyne had already talked at great length about her career with her parents and with Mr. and Mrs. Chisholm. It would be difficult for Mr. and Mrs. Price to pay for all the expenses of her advance study. Her brother George was already a student at South Carolina College at Orangeburg. He had entered as a freshman during Leontyne's senior year. The Prices were not able to send George through undergraduate school and pay for their daughter's graduate work at the same time.

The Prices are a proud family and never liked to feel indebted to anyone. But because of the way the Chisholms approached them, they agreed to accept their assistance. At that point Mrs. Chisholm told Leontyne she wouldn't have anything to worry about as far as financial aid was concerned.

One of the biggest events that took place in Leontyne's life, aside from the recognition she received whenever she travelled, occurred during her senior year. She sang on a program at Antioch College when Paul Robeson appeared there. Robeson was much impressed by her voice and observed that she was a very promising talent. He assured that if he could be of any assistance, he was anxious to help the career of this unusually gifted young singer.

Leontyne was highly excited about anyone making a contribution to her education. Several persons at the college decided to help Leontyne accept Robeson's offer. Dr. Anna Terry, Mr. Mack Green and Dr. Wesley realized that commencement was rapidly approaching and they were aware of Leontyne's aspirations for studying at Juilliard. However, Mr. Green and Dr. Terry contacted Mr. Robeson and inquired if he would be the main attraction at a concert in Dayton. The purpose was to establish a scholarship fund for Leontyne Price. The veteran concert singer readily accepted the request and a program was arranged for May 31, 1948 in Dayton's Memorial Hall. This marked the return of Paul Robeson to the local concert platform. He sang without charge to an overflow audience during commencement week. The event raised $1,000 and Leontyne was most grateful for Mr. Robeson's generosity. She also sang on the program and was deeply touched as she drew bravos for her own magnificent performance.

CHAPTER III

THE JUILLIARD SCHOOL OF MUSIC

When Leontyne Price arrived at the Juilliard School of Music it was already established that she possessed a big, colorful, vocal instrument, but it was still in an embryonic state. Much needed to be accomplished if it were to withstand the strains and demands of the competitive world of concerts and music drama. The young singer had already sung successfully with choral groups in high school and college. In addition, she had given moving concerts which showed vivid signs of promise. However, she lacked the much needed technique to pursue a lengthy career on the concert stage or in the world's most renowned operatic theatres.

Voice instruction began uneventfully for Leontyne when she enrolled at Juilliard in the fall of 1948. Mr. and Mrs. Chisholm financed her trip to New York and paid for her room and board as well as for the expenses of her books. By financially aiding Leontyne, they were not trying to take her away from her natural parents. They had a deep respect for Mr. and Mrs. Price and wanted to do all they could to help them.

Leontyne enrolled as just one among many aspiring students who had been carefully selected by a talent oriented faculty. One of her greatest strokes of good fortune was to be assigned with Florence Page Kimball for voice training. Her teacher, a former concert singer, had a deep sensitivity about the vocal needs of her students. She never rushed them and, consequently, enabled her pupils to develop at their own natural pace. "Quality comes with the luxury of time," Miss Kimball says when she refers to her own method of instruction. In order to do justice to them and to herself, she always limits the number of persons she takes at the time.

The amiable teacher wanted to do everything she could to help her new pupil. Although voice training was Leontyne's primary mission at Juilliard, she developed in her appearance. Simplicity was stressed in her manner of dress and in the way she carried herself. The temper that she had developed in earlier years was toned down considerably. Her mother very often had permitted her to have her way and, consequently, when she became displeased she would go into a tantrum.

When Leontyne first reported to her new teacher, Miss Kimball asked her what her name was. The uninhibited student responded:

"My name is Leontyne Price!"

"Child, don't you have another name, a simpler one?" asked the teacher.

"My mother calls me Mary," she answered.

Miss Kimball liked the second name much better than she did Leontyne and began to call her Mary.

Talent is the main prerequisite for admission to Juilliard. Therefore, it is not always possible for instructors to single out a real outstanding talent from the outset. Miss Kimball wanted a sampling of Leontyne's singing ability. The first song she heard was "Tu lo sai," an aria by Guiseppe Torelli. Miss Kimball was not too much impressed with her voice. She did not foresee a great future for Leontyne in the world of vocal music and proceeded with her as she did her other students.

However, Miss Kimball was immediately struck by her glittering charm. The novice singer was outgoing, lively and carefree. She made herself completely at home with Miss Kimball, most of the other students and the other members of the faculty. She felt completely at ease to discuss her personal problems with her teacher.

Back in Laurel she became an important member of the Chisholm family. Because of Leontyne, the Chisholm children sometimes got fewer or less expensive gifts at Christmastime. Their parents pointed out that they were contributing to their friend's professional training.

Mrs. Chisholm, deeply concerned about Leontyne's voice, visited Miss Kimball in her Manhattan apartment. Seated in her living room, she made inquiries about her protégé.

"You don't feel she has wonderful talent?" inquired Mrs. Chisholm with great concern.

"She has just started," Miss Kimball responded. "It is too early to tell."

Mrs. Chisholm's interest in Leontyne continued. She often visited her in New York and always made a report when she returned to Laurel.

During the summer months Leontyne returned home with her family. The Chisholms welcomed her visits and did not expect a detailed report on how much she had accomplished. She didn't sense any pressure or obligation to succeed. They helped her to develop added poise by putting her before an audience at every appropriate opportunity. She often sang for guests in the parlor of the Chisholm home as Mrs. Chisholm accompanied her on the piano.

Most of the out-of-town students who were enrolled at Juilliard lived at the International House. Conveniently located across the street from the school, it was an ideal setting for young aspirants in the arts. Living in this pleasant and relaxed atmosphere were students of countries from all over the world. This intermingling of persons of varied backgrounds and cultures was an education within itself. Leontyne not only took advantage of International House to enrich her personality, but also to perfect her art.

Very often, there was informal singing at International House. Students of the thirty or forty nations represented there, came together as close as they ever did each time Leontyne sang. In the walnut-panelled homeroom, they would gather around for the candlelit Sunday night suppers or concerts. Leontyne usually sang arias from the classics and would often close with folk songs or a spiritual such as "Ride on, King Jesus" or "Let Us Break Bread Together on Our Knees." Her singing, characterized by effortless grace, rarely left eyes dry when she had finished.

Shortly after Leontyne's arrival at Juilliard, she met Andrew Frierson. Andrew had already graduated from Juilliard and had taught one year at Southern University in Baton Rouge, Louisiana. He had returned to Juilliard for advanced study. Very often a group of students would congregate in one of Juilliard's practice rooms. As music students generally do, they liked to fool around with the piano and try out their vocal gifts. During one of their sessions Leontyne sang Bizet's "Agnus Dei." It was beautifully sung with deep feeling and sensitivity. This was the first time Andrew had heard Leontyne and he was very much impressed with her interpretation as well as her vocal talent. "You know it is just a matter of time for you, that's all, just time," he stated emphatically. He was convinced that she had an exceptional musical gift.

It was always fun when the Julliard students got together. Since most of them were from other cities, their common circumstances brought them even closer. Andrew Frierson resided in the home of Mrs. Victorine Kinloch, a really grand lady who lived on 124th Street. She very often welcomed a select group of music students for little musical soirées. Those "get-togethers" were amusing pastimes for the group. As most of the other students, Leontyne went over and sang just for the pleasure of it. They usually sang some of their classroom material. Some of them sang spirituals and others sang operatic arias. At times, some of them teamed up for duets.

There was an abundance of talent at Juilliard. Martha Flowers, Billie Lynn Daniel, Gloria Davy and Mary Robbs were among Leontyne's many friends and associates. Shortly after Leontyne arrived at the School, Andrew Frierson asked her to go out on a double date with him and Gloria Davy. She didn't have anyone to take her along and Andrew, therefore, made arrangements for William Hyatt, his best friend at Howard University, to come up from Washinghon, D. C., to accompany Leontyne.

The two couples went to the Royal Roost, a new thriving night spot located down on Broadway. Seated around the stage in bleachers, the foursome enjoyed an evening of entertainment featuring the talents of Harry Belafonte, an upcoming young calypso singer. The humorous Leontyne kept her friends in stitches all evening with jokes about herself and other persons.

Martha Flowers and Leontyne had a lot in common. Both were charming Southern girls and the two were hard-working young sopranos studying voice with Florence Page Kimball. They became very good friends and shared many of their interests together. Although Martha usually took off to the Bronx as soon as her classes were over, the students often found time to discuss their vocational ambitions.

Both young ladies loved to go to the movies together. Leontyne was especially fond of outstanding foreign films. One of her most memorable films was *Les Enfants du Paradis* that she saw with Martha at Manhattan's Thalia Theatre on upper Broadway.

Martha felt very close to Leontyne and was always grateful for her many generosities. Very often Martha did not have money to buy her meals and was ashamed to join Leontyne for lunch. On many occasions Leontyne would say to her: "Come on I'll treat you." She would pay for both lunches and didn't want Martha to feel embarrassed about it.

Leontyne, a serious student, kept her mind on her work. She and Martha studied songs for the repertory classes together. Their greatest fun, however, was in the make-up class. They laughed and joked about the problems they had because they were dark skinned and were given all shades of make-up that was traditionally used by white persons.

They found it strikingly funny when the instructor told the students how to make the nose look keener and give the cheeks and eyes a sunk-in appearance.

As most young ladies, they had crushes on some of the students at the School. They would go around and smile at them but were always too shy to say anything. Both girls liked Carl White and Samuel Kraetmalnick, but Leontyne had a special crush on Jean Morell. Martha tried unsuccessfully to persuade her to go up and say something to him.

The gregarious Leontyne finally fell in love with a young Haitian who resided in International House. He was engaged to a young Catholic girl back in Haiti and she knew it. He was shockingly handsome and his beige suits accentuated his beautiful black skin. The episode ended abruptly when he finally left her and got married. One night at a dance at International House she was dancing without her shoes on. Suddenly overcome by melancholy, she started out toward the Hudson River with the intention of committing suicide. A friend calmly suggested that she put her shoes back on first. She became indignant but reluctantly followed his instructions. He drove her across the George Washington Bridge while she had periodic fits of sobbing. After driving up and down the river most of the night, she returned to a normal state. Laughing about the incident in later years Leontyne said: "He was no musician, but he sure was an artist."

Martha Flowers and Mary Robbs were friends back at Fiske University in Nashville, Tennessee. Both young ladies studied voice there and had their sights set on New York City. After her graduation, Mary settled in the City and Martha came up the following year. Martha auditioned and was one of the fortunate ones to be accepted as a voice pupil of Florence Page Kimball. The black students, especially, adored Miss Kimball and she loved them dearly.

A deceptively powerful woman, Miss Kimball was noted for getting some of the best voices at the school. She was always very sweet and compassionate. Mary and Martha kept in close contact with each other. Whenever they talked Martha would say: "You must come to Juilliard and you must study with Miss Kimball."

Miss Kimball worked with Leontyne on the roles of *Aïda* and *Ariadne auf Naxos*. She also practiced isolated arias from other operas. She didn't want any talk of an operatic career too early because she felt that even the discussion of it would be harmful to Leontyne. She realized that Leontyne had lots of hard work ahead of her and that when she was properly prepared, the interested parties would seek her out. She tried to give Leontyne the material that was suitable for her vocal state rather than push her too fast. She coached her in voice, diction and *lieder*. Miss Kimball was anxious for her student to develop a good vocal technique.

After Leontine had been at Juilliard a year, she took part in a small concert given by some of the students. Miss Kimball invited Max Steiner to hear the performance. Earlier he had asked the teacher: "Do you know a good Bess?" Along with Alexander Smallens, he conducted the first Mamonlian production of *Porgy and Bess* back in 1936.

Steiner came up and heard Leontyne sing. Among other things, she sang some *zigeunerlieder*. During the concert he leaned over and wrote on the bottom of Miss Kimball's program: "She would be a good Bess." Mr. Steiner later sent Miss Kimball parts of the *Porgy and Bess* score and asked her to have Leontyne start working with it. "She should know it," he said. Leontyne studied it with Miss Kimball and when she returned to Laurel for her summer vacation, she continued her practice with Mrs. Chisholm.

While at Juilliard, Leontyne sang in the Riverside Church Choir. Richard Weagley, the choir director, auditioned her and put her in the choir with the rest of the singers. He didn't realize what a vocal gold mine he had at that time. Leontyne sang with the ensemble until she made other connections. Catherine Van Buren, her voice teacher back at Wilberforce, had settled in New York City and was singing with the choir. During one of their desultory conversations, Leontyne mentioned to her former teacher about some difficulty she was having with her pianissimo tones. She wanted to perfect the method that is needed to control the volume of the voice, maintaining richness and vibrancy, and at the same time carrying a pianissimo. Miss Van Buren was not teaching at the time and, regretfully, was unable to help her. However, she advised Leontyne as best she could and steered her in the right direction.

Vocal training is an expensive ordeal. Many of the students had to take church jobs in order to eke out an existence while in music school. Some found work in Harlem or in other communities in the New York Metropolitan area. They never ceased to grab these opportunities as soon as they became available. Leontyne was looked upon as the Cinderella of the school. Not only did she have an outstanding talent, she had so many other things in her favor. She always appeared to have adequate financial support. Although she never seemed pressed for money for her basic needs, she, too, worked while attending Juilliard.

She secured employment on the information desk at International House. She earned enough money to take care of some of her personal needs such as expenses for opera performances and for the movies.

Although Leontyne had thought about singing in grand opera back at Wilberforce, she really got set on it after she came to New York. She was determined to become an opera singer despite the fact that most roles in the standard repertory that were usually considered "suitable" for black female singers were limited.

The first performance of opera she heard was Puccini's *Turandot* at the City Center in New York City. Later, she stood up at the Metropolitan Opera House to hear a production of *Salome*. After the performance of *Salome*, she was totally convinced that she wanted to pursue a career in grand opera. She then said in silence: "I have got to be an opera singer."

Leontyne wanted to be somebody. She had a tremendous drive to be a success and was determined not to fail. It was extremely difficult to get into the Juilliard Opera Workshop because of the keen competition among so many talented students. There is usually a limitation of students in an active workshop and one, therefore, must have outstanding qualities to be accepted. Some students had to wait as long as three years before being accepted at Juilliard. Leontyne, prompted by her burning desire to sing opera, auditioned and was fortunate enough to get in during her second year.

Frederic Cohen was director of Juilliard's Opera Department. After hearing her sing for the first time, he went home and told his wife: "We have the voice of the century." She had sung the "Lament" from *Dido and Aeneas* in his Introduction to Opera course. She had sung it freely and with exceptional feeling. "I had no doubt from the first moment that she could make the grade," he said.

Leontyne got into as many opera productions as she could. In her first role, she sang the role of Aunt Nella in *Gianni Schicchi*. At that time she did not have adequate experience to sing the part of Laurette, the principal female role.

In 1951 Clift Roberts, a friend of the Chisholms, planned a small private birthday party for Dwight D. Eisenhower at the Park Lane. Eisenhower was then President of Columbia University. Mr. Roberts had already heard Leontyne and asked her to sing at his party. Miss Kimball felt that something was developing for Leontyne and wanted her to accept and to just be herself. Dressed in a simple green dress, the young singer gladly appeared to sing. She included among her selections "We Like Ike" from *Call Me Madam*, the Broadway musical. She got all the men to join in the second chorus. Later she said very calmly: "They asked me to sing, and I did. That's about all there was to it. It was just a small party."

The opera was presented in Juilliard's one thousand-seat Recital Hall on February 20, 22 and 23, 1952. The singers had been rehearsing their parts since the preceding fall. Miss Price was unaffected about being the only member of her race in the cast. She sang her role without the use of facial makeup scoring a resounding success. Backed by a corps of splendid voices and a soundly trained orchestra, she was launched into a professional career.

It was a public performance and for the first time Robert Breen, Blevins Davis and Virgil Thompson heard Miss Price sing. Davis and Breen were talent searching for an upcoming production of *Porgy and Bess*. Howard Taubman, critic for the *New York Times* observed: "Miss Price has a rich, well-placed dramatic voice, and she knows how to use it."

Mr. Breen, very much impressed with Leontyne's voice, concluded that she would be an excellent Bess. However, he did nothing about it immediately. Meanwhile, Virgil Thomson was engaged in mounting a Paris revival of *Four Saints in Three Acts* for the 1952 International Arts Festival. He offered Leontyne the role of Saint Cecelia.

Betty Allen went to New York to audition for a John Whitney Fellowship. While there she learned that Virgil Thomson was looking for a Saint Theresa Two and the company was going to Paris. At that time Betty had changed from a soprano to a mezzo-soprano. She happily accepted the part of Saint Theresa Two. Billie Lynn Daniel, Gloria Davy and Olga James were some of the outstanding members of the chorus. Martha Flowers sang the role of Saint Settlement.

Thompson was so impressed with Leontyne's voice that he wrote in a little part especially for her. She had an opportunity to really show off her voice by going very high up the scale. To balance it up, he gave a small part to Ida Johns who had a very deep contralto voice. Ida did a scale going down while Leontyne went up very high. In the extremely demanding role of Saint Cecelia, Leontyne outclassed all her colleagues. Leontyne also understudied for Aenis Matthews who was Saint Theresa One. The former had a bigger voice but the latter had a more flourishing career.

It is often said in music circles that if a singer has good diction, it's because he has had an "attack of Virgil Thomson at an early age." When Virgil was asked why he used Negroes for the 1952 revival of the opera, he said: "Because Negroes have such marvelous diction." He also said they have the most unusually credible faith which is visible on stage. Virgil felt that they could play the parts of saints and make it seem like they believed everything they said and did. The ability to project this feeling was what made all the characters so interesting in that production.

It had been intended for *Four Saints in Three Acts* to run indefinitely in New York. In the interim, Robert Breen approached Miss Kimball about having Leontyne audition for the role of Bess. The teacher refused to talk to her student about it because she felt that Leontyne had to honor her commitment with Virgil Thomson. She thought, however, that the role of Bess would be a wonderful opportunity for Leontyne. Ultimately, Leontyne made her own decision. She personally did not do anything that violated her agreement with the *Four Saints* Company.

After two weeks on Broadway, something went wrong with *Four Saints in Three Acts* and the production closed down. There was a few weeks' lapse before it was scheduled to leave for Paris. During the interim, Leontyne auditioned for the role of Bess, got signed up and began rehearsals for the part.

In 1961 Nicholas Nobokov suggested Leontyne for the summer festival at Tanglewood. She was engaged for the second and third acts of *Aïda*. Boris Goldovsky was head of the Opera School of the Berkshire Music Center. They participated in short scenes, acts from operas and also complete operas.

At that time the Berkshire Festival consisted of two

separate organizations. One was the Boston Symphony and the other was the Berkshire Music Center which was a six-week summer school for advanced students. Leontyne was auditioned among many others and was accepted in the Opera School. When she arrived there she met up with Betty Allen, her good friend back at Wilberforce. Both were scholarship students: Leontyne was in the opera department and Betty was a chorus leader.

Operatically speaking, Leontyne was still a "greenhorn." That summer the major production was Tchaikovsky's *Queen of Spades* which was presented with the orchestra. However, *Ariadne auf Naxos* was also given but was done with piano accompaniment. Leontyne sang the leading role of the latter work which was presented in English. She made a considerable impression with her singing. Until that moment, she was thought of merely as just another soprano student of the school. But in that performance, she made it decidedly clear that she had something unusual both in her vocal equipment and in her stage personality.

Leontyne worked very hard for three years at Juilliard. She didn't trample on anyone to get ahead, nor did she let anything stand in her way as she strived diligently toward her goal. Her vocal gifts continued to unravel as she developed technique. She was in her fourth year when the Juilliard Opera Theatre selected Verdi's *Falstaff* for its big production effort of the year.

This comic opera, written as Verdi was approaching eighty years of age, is a unique masterpiece. It is a difficult work to produce even by the world's veteran opera houses. The score of the opera calls for *Falstaff*, sung by Orville White, to make love to Mistress Ford. Frederic Cohen selected Leontyne Price for the leading female role on the basis of her auditions which were held along with the other students.

CHAPTER IV

PORGY AND BESS

When Robert Breen and Blevins Davis announced the revival of *Porgy and Bess* in 1952, the title roles went to William Warfield and Leontyne Price. The folk opera based on *Porgy*, the Dorothy and Dubose Heyward play, had not been done since the Cheryl Crawford production. Brilliantly mounted with intensely dramatic staging, it was the fifth *Porgy and Bess* scheduled to appear on Broadway since the original opening in 1935.

The original *Porgy and Bess*, with music by George Gershwin, was done in its entirety and was much too operatic for Broadway. Presented by the Theatre Guild, it was not a great success. Later Cheryl Crawford produced it taking out all the operatic material leaving only the songs which were bound together with dialogue. It then became a big hit on Broadway.

Blevins Davis and Robert Breen began to restore as much of the music as possible and also added music never used before. They juxtaposed several things like the Buzzard Song which had been left out entirely and put it in the last scene just when Porgy gets back home as an omen to him. Still, however, a lot of dialogue was left in and a lot of ad libbing. The unique touch-up job done by Messieurs Breen and Davis and an abundance of extraordinary talent made the 1952 version by far the best of the five.

Leontyne was relatively unknown but Bill was one of the best known singers of the day. A graduate of the Eastman School of Music at the University of Rochester in the State of New York, he returned there after a three and a half year stint in the Army. He wanted to get a Master of Arts Degree in musical literature to prepare for a teaching career. His voice showed clear signs of promise and he was cast with the road company of the Broadway smash hit *Call Me Mister,* in 1947. He also appeared with great success in *Set My People Free* and *Regina,* a piano-playing and singing act in night clubs. Bill had also scored a success in the latest screen version of *Show Boat* with Kathryn Grayson.

Up to that point, Leontyne had made her most dramatic step forward theatrically in Virgil Thompson's *Four Saints in Three Acts.* Shortly after she had been contracted to sing the role of Bess, Bill immediately went over on Broadway to get a taste of what her voice was like. "I was tremendously impressed," he commented later. *Four Saints* took off for Paris and Bill didn't get to hear her again until the first days of the rehearsals.

Leontyne had attended Bill Warfield's debut at Town Hall while she was a student at Juilliard. She was hoping to get a chance to meet him in person but was unable to fathom her way through the crowds. The debut created quite a stir in the press for Bill. He got a contract to go to Australia for a three-month tour. He was then signed up with André Mertens' division at Columbia Artists Management, Incorporated.

The rehearsals for *Porgy and Bess* began in May 1952. They took place up in Harlem in a big loft upstairs over a store on 125th Street and Seventh Avenue. At that point Bill and Lee really began to know each other. After they started working together, Bill discovered that her performance as Bess was going to completely eclipse what he had originally heard in *Four Saints.* There was just so much there vocally that wasn't evident when he heard her sing the small part earlier on Broadway.

Bill was ecstatic about this new singer who was to share the title role with him. The next time he was with Larney Goodkind, his manager, he said, "We've got two Besses in this company. They're going to alternate performances. One of them has the most wonderful voice. You really have to hear her."

Larney Goodkind and his wife went up to Harlem for one of the rehearsals. When they arrived, Alexander Smallens, the conductor, had already begun giving instructions to the accompanist who was using a mini-piano. Seated nearby was Florence Page Kimball, Leontyne's teacher. When Bill and Lee sang the famous duet "Bess, You Is My Woman Now," tears began to come to the eyes of most of the listeners. It was beautifully done from every point of view: vocally, musically and emotionally. Members of the cast as well as the other listeners were awed by what they were hearing. The Goodkinds, hearing Leontyne for the first time, immediately fell in love with her voice.

Shortly after the rehearsals started, Bill and Leontyne began dating each other. One evening he arranged to take her out with Larney Goodkind and his wife. They had dinner over at Sardi's, Broadway's celebrated theatrical rendezvous. Afterwards, they went to the Goodkinds' apartment in Manhattan's Chelsea district. A mutual friend of Larney and Bill joined the two couples for fun, games and an interesting discussion of music.

"How about singing some Brahms' songs?" Bill suddenly asked Leontyne. "I'll play for you," he said.

She gladly fulfilled his request and Mr. and Mrs. Goodkind were quite struck with hearing her sing a different form of music for the first time. Bill then persuaded his date to do her famous imitation of Sarah Vaughn. The Goodkinds were impressed and amused by her interpretation. They were especially delighted with her musicianship and her potentials as an artist.

Porgy and Bess first opened in Dallas, Texas. When Leontyne hit the stage in a flamboyant red dress and a Carmen-like red rose in her hair, the stage automatically became alive. She had pure animal drive. The role of Bess requires a tremendous kind of projected animalistic acting ability and yet it also requires a very cultured type of singing to be able to negotiate the kind of tones in singing the duet and in the reprise of the "Summertime" with the high floating A. Usually when one finds somebody who has that kind of vocal quality, the other animalistic acting ability is lacking. Leontyne was a perfect combination of the two of them. In sum, she was a definitive Bess.

In the audience was Mrs. Elizabeth Chisholm accompanied by about twenty of her friends. Leontyne's brother George was also present. He had completed his studies at South Carolina State College and had been wounded in Korea where he had served as a lieutenant in the Infantry.

As in other southern cities, racial discrimination was practiced in Dallas. However, the members of the cast managed to avoid it. They were lodged in private homes or in a motel which was reserved for Negroes. They stayed too busy to go anywhere or do anything not related to the performance. Most of their travelling was done by taxi.

Bill decided to rent a car and had the producer call and arrange for him to get it. When he returned, some of the other fellows in the cast thought it was a very good idea to have a car while in Dallas. They went down to rent one also, but were refused. They came back infuriated because they had been denied an automobile. The producer called down and straightened it out and they too were granted car rental privileges.

Before the performance Mrs. Chisholm had attended a rehearsal and later strolled with Leontyne toward her hotel. The doorman stopped them saying it was restricted to whites only. Mrs. Chisholm gave him a good tongue lashing and summoned the manager. In a short time the two women were lunching together in Mrs. Chisholm's hotel suite.

Chicago was the next stop for the *Porgy and Bess* Company. Then it went to Pittsburgh and later opened in Washington, D. C. Larney Goodkind and his wife went to the opening night in Chicago. When they arrived at the hotel, they got a message to call Mr. Warfield's room.

When Larney got him on the phone he said:

"Hi, we're here!"

"Yeah," said Bill excitedly. "Would you know how to go about getting a diamond ring?"

"What?" exclaimed Larney.

"An engagement ring," said Bill.

"You're kidding."

"No, I'm not," answered Bill.

Bill started to laugh, but Larney began to sense his sincerity about being engaged.

One of the women connected with the *Porgy and Bess* company recommended a jeweler. Between press parties and other activities, Larney and his wife assisted Bill in selecting a ring.

That night Bill and Leontyne, along with the Goodkinds, had dinner together in one of the restaurants at the Hotel Sherman. The young couple became officially engaged when Bill presented the ring to her.

Bill telephoned Mrs. Price to give her the news about his engagement to her daughter. She wanted to know if the marriage was going to end Leontyne's career.

"No," said Bill. "I am perfectly willing for Leontyne to keep on with it, go abroad, and give lots of concerts."

"Oh," said Mrs. Price, "and what are you going to be doing?"

"I'll be singing too," answered the future son-in-law.

Mrs. Price knew that her daughter was strong-willed and had to be directed. "You tell her what she must do. Be the man. You've got to take her in hand and control her. She's used to having her way. Just take over," said the concerned mother.

Bill's parents got to Chicago to see *Porgy and Bess* before it moved on to Washington. They also had the opportunity of meeting Leontyne for the first time. In Washington the company performed at the National Theatre. President Harry S. Truman was the guest of honor. The theatre had been closed for a long period of time because its managment had refused to permit Negroes in the audience or as members of the casts.

Music critic David Hume wrote: "Leontyne Price sings the most exciting and thrilling Bess we have heard . . . Price will no doubt spend a long time in the role of Bess. But when she is available for other music she will have a dramatic career. And her acting is as fiery as her singing."

Bill and Lee decided to have a big wedding at Bill's church, Abyssinian Baptist Church in New York City. Larney Goodkind and his wife had to handle all the arrangements because the young couple was performing in Washington. When Leontyne wanted to buy clothes for her wedding in Washington and couldn't try them on at Julius Garfinkel and Company because of the store's segregated policies, Mrs. Chisholm had her friend, Mrs. Charles "Chip" Bohlen, give a garden party with models from Garfinkels'. Leontyne was very much impressed and thought of it as a big ball. When she got back with Bill and the *Porgy and Bess* cast, she said: "I got out there and all of a sudden I looked around and there were all those models, modeling these gowns. The rich do live mighty, don't they?"

The final performance of *Porgy and Bess* in the nation's capital was on a Saturday night and the wedding was scheduled for the following day. Mr. Warfield engaged a bus for all the members of the cast who wanted to attend the ceremonies. The bus left Washington early Sunday morning to arrive in time for the wedding in the afternoon of August 31, 1952. Mr. Warfield and his fiancée had gone up to New York the preceding night. The chartered bus, carrying the cast plus the parents of the bride-to-be, got stuck in some deep water and had several blowouts. It was on a weekend and the company did not rent them one of its best vehicles. However, it finally arrived just in time for the wedding.

Dr. Adam Clayton Powell, Jr., was planning to perform the ceremonies. He was out on Long Island on the day of the wedding and was planning to drive into town. Everything was prepared for his arrival, but about an hour before the ritual he telephoned saying that his new car had broken down and he was stranded. His assistant, Dr. Licorice, replaced him. Bill's father, Reverend Robert E. Warfield, pastor of the Mount Vernon Baptist Church in Rochester, assisted him. The six bridesmaids were members of the *Porgy and Bess* cast.

Following the ceremonies, a big reception took place at the Theresa Hotel located several blocks from the church. The wedding cake was topped by a musical staff with the first notes of "Bess, You Is My Woman Now."

Immediately after the wedding the cast went back to Washington to leave for Vienna the following day. Bill and Leontyne were going to take the bus back with the other members of the cast but their friends got together and decided that it would be too pressing for the newlyweds and that they should get back earlier to make preparations for the departure. As a friendly gesture the cast presented them with plane tickets back to Washington.

The bus had problems again on the return trip. The cast was stranded all night and did not arrive in the nation's capital until the next morning. The bus broke down on the road for several hours with flat tires and had all kinds of other problems.

The same day of arrival in Washington, they took off for Europe in Military Air Transport Service planes. The State Department insisted that the tour be interrupted and be shown in Vienna, Berlin, London and Paris for good will. The whole thing was a real madhouse. They got almost half way out over the Atlantic and something went wrong. They had not gone past the "point of no return" so the plane turned around and headed back. Leontyne was fast asleep. Bill, completely aware of what was going on, decided not to disturb his bride.

When the plane was almost ready to land Leontyne woke up and said: "Oh, we are landing!"

"Yes, in Washington," said Bill.

"What?" she said.

She probably would have been in an hysterical fit had she known earlier what was happening, but Bill just let her sleep. The plane returned to Washington, got repaired and made its second takeoff.

Since the cast was not travelling in a commercial airliner, the Viennese could not get any information about what had happened to the *Porgy and Bess* cast. When they did not arrive as scheduled, rumors had already begun to circulate that they had gone down in the Atlantic and that the plane had disappeared.

In Switzerland, a year or more earlier, a production of *Porgy and Bess* had been done in blackface. A very blond, blue-eyed girl came up to Bill backstage and said, "I have done Bess. I was Bess. I played the role of Bess." She presented a very horrible picture of herself to Bill. She was all made up for the role of Bess. Although the makeup wasn't good, she was just enthralled and wanted the cast to see pictures of her in costume and in her blackface.

After waiting seventeen years for the opportunity of seeing a performance of *Porgy and Bess,* the Londoners adored it. The opera opened a private run at the Stoll Theatre. The vast and ornate auditorium overflowed its seating capacity of 2,500. About nine hundred disappointed persons were turned away. The American community, headed by Ambassador Walter Gifford, was there in large numbers. At the end of the performance, there was a long ovation punctuated by roars of "bravos" for the principal singers, Leontyne Price and William Warfield.

The cast encountered no racial prejudice in Europe. At first some of them had a very hard time getting living accommodations in London. If they went to inquire about a place of lodging that had been advertised, all of a sudden they were informed that it had been taken. When the news reached the press, the English were lambasted for this attitude. It stated that racial intolerance would not be condoned. The problems began to fade. People got enraged at the thought of this unpleasant situation and began to call in offering apartments.

Eventually everybody got located. Bill and Leontyne got a nice flat in South West Kensington. They shared it with one of the lead baritones of the company and his wife. There was no central heating and they had to get adjusted to the idea of using fireplaces. The bathroom was kept warm by the hot water fixtures running through it. Bill absolutely hated London at first. Too much was involved to keep their flat warm. If they were cooking in the kitchen, they would make a fire in the living room. The fire in the bedroom had to be banked and started again the next day.

Although Bill hated London when he first arrived, he began to like it after he had been there a month. By prior agreement, he had to return to New York in December of 1952. By that time he was settled and had become a real Londoner, but he had to leave the show to fulfill concert agreements arranged by Columbia Artists. He was expected to rejoin the cast in May of the next year in time for the Coronation of Queen Elizabeth II which took place in June.

In January 1953 while the show was in Paris, Leontyne wrote to Larney Goodkind asking him if he would consider taking her on for personal management. She expressed how happy she would be if he could just do for her what he had done for William Warfield. "I'd like to join the family," she said. Bill had already discussed this with his wife in Europe and Goodkind was very pleased to accept Leontyne. He immediately drew up a suitable contract for her.

Larney was entrusted with handling all her funds. He took out a joint bank account with her as he had done with Warfield. All of the money earned came through him. Larney sent monthly checks to Mr. and Mrs. Price in accordance with Leontyne's request. Sometimes he would say to her:

"Leontyne, won't you take this check book and look it over?"

"What for?" she would say. "I trust you completely. There's nothing for me to look at or see. There are just a lot of figures and it will get my head all whirled and there's no reason."

It was originally planned for the show to run in London through most of the summer of 1963. Preparations were made for it to open at the Metropolitan Opera House in New York preceding the opera season, but business began to fall off. Billy Rose saw it in London and thought it was a great show. He still had his Ziegfeld Theatre back in New York which was empty at the time. Billy offered the management special rental terms for his theatre and said: "Bring it to New York now in March—don't wait." Rose, an astute businessman, was anxious to fill his theatre.

By agreement of Breen and Davis, Rose came back to the States and tried to persuade Goodkind to have Warfield break his contract so that Bill and Lee could open together in his theatre.

"Mr. Warfield is very strict about one thing among others, and that is a contract," said Goodkind. "That's his bond, that's his word. He will not go back on that. He feels he'd be breaking faith with people who wanted him and made these contracts. And he won't do that."

"Oh, I can get him out of these contracts," said Rose.

"He doesn't want to get out of anything. If he can open in *Porgy and Bess* and go on with commitments too—fine. But if he can't, the *Porgy* will have to wait."

Rose began to get very nasty on the phone. "I know these people up at Columbia Artists. I'll get them to change," he snapped.

"It can't be done," answered Goodkind.

All of a sudden Rose, annoyed and frustrated, said: "I'm sitting here at my desk staring at sixteen inches of Daumier that's worth ten Warfields."

"Well, good for you," said Goodkind very calmly.

The producers tried unsuccessfully to have Bill open in *Porgy and Bess* at the Ziegfeld between concerts and then go back to complete his commitments. They were anxious for his name to appear in the opening night reviews.

"That's not playing good faith with theatregoers in New York who read the reviews and then buy tickets and find that he isn't in it," said Larney Goodkind.

When the Breen-Davis production of *Porgy and Bess* opened at the Ziegfeld, obviously missing from the original cast was William Warfield. However, Leslie Scott who shared the title role with Leontyne, made a memorable impression on the press.

The acting and singing of the completely refreshed production was superb. "As Bess," wrote Brooks Atkinson in the *New York Times*, "Leontyne Price sings with rapture and professional skill and acts with fire and abandon, turning that wayward part into a new person."

Bill's concert tour finally ended on May 4 and he was free to come back to join the *Porgy and Bess* cast. However, at that point the management refused to take him. He had a run of the play contract which would pay him through June 1. He was paid his salary for the few remaining weeks, but he never sang with Leontyne in that production in New York City.

The producers of *Porgy and Bess* arranged schedules so that Leontyne could take off to do special concerts. During this time Samuel Barber entered her life for the first time professionally. Barber, who had half completed his "Hermit Songs" in 1953, said:

"After I heard Leontyne Price sing, I more or less wrote the balance of the songs for her."

Mr. Barber accompanied her when she sang them for the first time in the Library of Congress in Washington, D. C., that year and again at the 20th Century Music Conference in Rome. He also accompanied her when she made her Town Hall debut. "The same year, I was also responsible for her debut performance with the Boston Symphony in the premier of my *Prayers of Kierkegaard*. I wanted her for this and asked Mr. Munch to get her. I admire her very much. She brought something very rich and very southern to my *Knoxville: Summer* of 1915, when Thomas Schippers conducted it for her."

Also in 1953, she was invited by such other notable musicians as Stravinsky, Lou Harrison, Henri Sauget, William Killmayer and John LaMontaine to premiere their works under such diverse auspices as the Museum of Modern Art, the Metropolitan Museum of Art and the Fromm Foundation.

Leontyne was with the *Porgy and Bess* Company exactly two years. The producers were unhappy when she left although they realized that she had a career to get on with. There wasn't that much to gain artistically by just playing and singing the role of Bess over and over again.

There was a lot of excitement about Leontyne's run with *Porgy and Bess* at the Ziegfeld. When she made her Town Hall debut in 1953, a lot of people went to hear her mainly to see how she would bridge the gap between the role of Bess and more serious music. It was almost like going from musical comedy to grand opera. The reviews were mixed, but she came out unscathed.

CHAPTER V

AMERICAN OPERATIC DEBUTS
NBC OPERA

The role of *Tosca* has played a significant part in the spectacular career of Leontyne Price. It marked her professional debut in grand opera, not only on the television screen, but in an operatic theatre as well. Reaching millions of enthusiastic viewers, her interpretation of the title role brought her nationwide acclaim.

When Leontyne was first telecast as Tosca by the National Broadcasting Company Opera Theatre in January, 1955, she was relatively unknown to the world of music drama. Large numbers of opera buffs did not remember her. Less than three years previously, she had begun rehearsals for her strikingly dramatic appearances in *Porgy and Bess* with William Warfield. The first major break was to take her on tours for two years in several cities of the United States and Europe.

Conductor Peter Herman Adler, musical director of the NBC-TV Opera, remembered her well. Having seen and heard her interpretation of Bess, he knew she could act. Also, the tones of her glorious voice still lingered. Although Leontyne was successful in the role of Bess, she never thought of musical comedy as a career. Her ambition was always to sing grand opera. For her, Bess was just a stepping stone in that direction which was first afforded by NBC.

When Mr. Adler first heard Leontyne in a performance of *Porgy and Bess*, he was particularly impressed by the long good-bye to Porgy before Bess takes off for the picnic.

Price sang a sustained pianissimo which went down to nothing. Adler "just went out of his seat." John Gutman's English version of *Tosca*, the Puccini opera, was to be presented by NBC in January, 1955. Mr. Adler immediately thought of her as a possible Floria Tosca.

Conductor Adler realized that there would be a great risk in casting a Negro singer in so outstanding a white role in a television presentation. However, he auditioned her as he did any other talented individual. He was so pleased with what he had heard that he took her to Producer Samuel Chotzinoff's office at NBC.

It was in the summertime and Leontyne, wearing a blue checked dress, seated herself and awaited her next date with destiny. Though sweet and innocent, the twenty-six-year-old soprano was most charming. She didn't know what was going to come from this encounter. At that point she was completely unaware of all the things that had to be considered and discussed about the difficulties involving the Southern stations.

The young soprano remained relatively calm, but somewhat frightened at the serious look on Mr. Chotzinoff's face. After observing her carefully, he asked her to sing two arias. She sang so convincingly that in ten minutes there was no question at all about taking the risk of casting her as *Tosca*.

Mr. Chotzinoff commented: "This is the sound we want, and we're pleased to have you with us, Miss Price, and we hope you will be pleased working with us. You will be a wonderful Tosca."

Although Mr. Adler and Mr. Chotzinoff were both in agreement, the final answer had to be given by David Sarnoff, president of NBC. It was a delicate decision to make. Mr. Chotzinoff went upstairs to consult with Mr. Sarnoff. He asked him if it would be permitted to cast Miss Price in the role.

"Is she a good singer?" he asked.

"She's a great singer," Chotzinoff responded.

"That's all you have to think about," said Mr. Sarnoff.

Making arrangements with Leontyne was a very simple matter for NBC, but other problems developed for the station. Eleven of its affiliates in the South rejected the show because of the appearance of Leontyne Price with a white cast. The soprano did not learn of the difficulties until the whole thing was finished. The management felt that there was no need to cause her to worry. She appeared as a Negro with no white makeup. "I was the first black Tosca that big audience had seen," she said.

On January 24, 1955, Paul Hume gave his opinion of Miss Price's interpretation of the role in the *Washington Post and Times Herald*. "In the title role the producers had the imagination, for she had never sung opera before, to put Leontyne Price, the superb American soprano whose steady rise to the top is one of the exciting things about our musical life these days. Vocally, Miss Price is a Tosca for the opera house of whatever gods may love opera. She can sail into those big fat phrases and make them rise with a beauty that is both strong and controlled.

"To watch her in the tricky business that fills the Bernhardt-famous role, is to see no false move, no empty gesture. It is true that certain motions of the head were unimpressive because of the TV camera at that moment, but they were the right moves for Tosca.

"And in her facial miming and her bodily motility, Price is a Tosca who can change from pitifully imploring to feral fury in an instant. Her magnificent climactic scene with Scarpia had a burning rage few sopranos hint at. She is a stunning, sumptuous sounding Tosca, and ought quickly to follow Marian Anderson's lead into the Metropolitan."

Cavaradossi was sung by David Poleri. He was one of Leontyne's old friends from Juilliard who used to sing in the lobby with her back at the International House.

The officials at NBC said they chose Miss Price not to break racial barriers, but because she was "the very best Tosca we could find." The young soprano's success was beyond all expectations. Her quietly expressive acting began to come across to a nationwide audience. She became the coquettish young Floria Tosca in the arms of Cavaradossi, her handsome lover.

Time Magazine wrote: "Vocally, she was head and shoulders above the others, crooning pearly high notes, dropping into gutty dramatic tones there. She sang the great second-act aria, "Vissi d'arte" with a flair worthy of the Met."

Olin Downes, famous critic of the *New York Times*, commented: "Miss Price, none too well costumed in the first act, nor as yet an experienced and finished actress, surmounted these obstacles by her remarkable voice, her native intelligence and sincerity and her growing freedom and effectiveness as the opera progressed.

"The voice became freer, fuller and richer with each scene," he continued. "Miss Price never sought to obtrude her equipment as a singer upon the development of the drama, of which she sought at all times to be a component part. . . . in the aria of supplication in the second act—the one familiar in the words of the Italian text, 'Vissi d'Arte'— she sang it gloriously, coloring her tones in a delivery as unaffected as it was communicative."

NBC-TV not only discovered a new artist, but continued to present her in other operas. She premiered Poulenc's *Dialogues of the Carmelites*. She later sang in Mozart's *Magic Flute* and in his *Don Giovanni*. The latter work was repeated by popular demand.

It was in January 1956 that Miss Price sang in the NBC televised production of *The Magic Flute*. In its commentary on this beautifully sung color spectable *Time Magazine* wrote: "Top singer in a high-flying cast was Leontyne Price, whose liquid soprano never sounded truer or sweeter."

"When I heard her sing the music of Pamina I knew that her voice and her art were part of the keystone of my life and mind. Her instinct for Mozart is preternatural," wrote Marcia Davenport about Leontyne Price in her book entitled *Too Strong for Fantasy*.

Televiewers throughout the United States had an opportunity to draw their conclusions, too, about Miss Price's interpretation of Pamina when the NBC Opera Theatre presented *The Magic Flute*. Written during the last year of Mozart's life, the production was presented to a huge television audience. The Mozartean work was a tribute to the composer's 200th birthday which occurred on January 27, 1956.

Considered one of the most difficult of operas, it contains some of the composer's loveliest music. It was presented in good taste by a youthful company which included John Reardon who sang Papageno, Laurel Hurley as the Queen of the Night, and William Lewis as Tamino. The cast was well supported by a sizable chorus and members of the Symphony of the Air under the expert direction of Peter Herman Adler.

When Miss Price appeared on the telecast, it was the first time she had been cast in the role of Pamina. In his appraisal of Miss Price's performance, Howard Taubman wrote in the *New York Times* on January 15, 1956: "Leontyne Price sang Pamina with a beauty of tone and purity of style that should have satisfied the most exacting of Mozartians."

THE SAN FRANCISCO OPERA

In the world of music drama, impresarios make a neverending search for new vocal talent. They pride themselves in being the first one to engage promising singers who live up to their expected standards. Included among a corps of great singers who have made their American debuts with the San Francisco Opera Company are Birgit Nilsson, Elizabeth Schwarzkoff, Renata Tabaldi, Mario del Monaco, Jess

Thomas, Tito Gobbi and Sandor Konya.

Kurt Herbert Adler of San Francisco's War Memorial Opera House can boast of being the one who engaged Leontyne Price for her first performance in a major opera house. Mr. Adler, the general manager, met Leontyne when she went to San Francisco to appear in Francis Poulenc's *Dialogues of the Carmelites*. After her first triumphant telecast by the NBC Opera Theatre, she became a constant topic of discussion in music circles. When her name was added to the roster, it was her on stage professional debut in grand opera.

Poulenc, having been impressed by her concert performances of his songs, was delighted for Miss Price to appear in his opera when it was presented in the United States. This moving opera on the triumph of faith over fear had recently received its world premiere at La Scala in Milan, Italy.

Dialogues of the Carmelites involves the fate of an order of nuns who were caught up in the French Revolution. Leontyne, cast as Madame Lidoine, sang the role of a baker's daughter who bypassed an aristocratic nun to become a prioress in a nunnery. The stage was swarming with nuns, but Leontyne stood out like a beacon. Although the debut was a major success, Miss Price "enjoyed a real cold petrification."

In the middle of the intermission, during a performance of *The Dialogues,* Mr. Adler approached Leontyne suddenly with a strange expression on his face. "Miss Antonietta Stella has cancelled for an emergency appendectomy," he said. Everything was ready for *Aïda* with no one to sing the part. Leontyne was asked if she knew it and she answered affirmatively. Having learned it earlier, she had sung it in concert form with the Philadelphia Orchestra without costumes. She sang it again later with Eugene Ormandy at the Ann Arbor, Michigan, Spring Festival.

The next thing she knew, she was on the stage to sing the title role in *Aïda*. "I can't go wrong," she said to herself.

"This'll be the first time I've ever been on a stage for this kind of thing, and let's face it, my skin was in my favor for a change. I got that made. I can't lose! There's nothing to worry about."

There was no problem of her making herself heard because Maestro Francesco Molinari-Pradelli, the conductor, is not heavy handed with the baton. The only thing she was really concerned about was getting on the wrong side of the stage. Although she didn't know where she was going, she tried to give the impression that she did.

"I can't go wrong," she kept saying to herself. When the Ethiopian slaves came in she'd just go wherever they went. Her biggest problem was to find out the location of the tomb. Between each act she walked up to the director saying: "Maestro, where . . .?" He acted as if he wasn't listening and said: "You were wonderful; you are beautiful tonight; and you just go change the costume and it's going to be fine."

"I have a question to ask you," she finally said. "Where is the tomb? Where am I going to die? I don't have the slightest idea where I am going to die!" The maestro burst into laughter. However, the new Aïda did find the tomb. It was the night of September 20, 1957, and Leontyne Price began her triumphal march across the world's renowned operatic stages.

Customarily, the fancy dressed operagoers who assemble at the theatre on Tuesday and Friday nights are cooler in their reception of artists than the audiences that come on other evenings, but that Friday's listeners behaved as if they were not wearing their white ties and Christian Dior gowns. They cheered and stomped and almost went out of their minds giving Miss Price one of the most impressive ovations of that season.

Kurt Herbert Adler was determined to expand her artistic and vocal range and cast her in a variety of roles in subsequent seasons. He had her sing Donna Elvira in *Don Giovanni* with the San Francisco Opera Company. On

September 26, 1958, she sang the role of Leonora for the first time in her career at the War Memorial Opera House. Critic Alexander Field of the *Examiner* said it was "an unforgettable performance," while Jussi Bjoerling as Manrico "gave a performance worthy of his renown." When Leontyne finished singing her great aria at the beginning of the last act, conductor Georges Sebastian threw down his baton and led the stunned audience in the applause.

On October 3, 1958, Carl Orff's *The Wise Maiden* was given its American premiere on a double-bill with the American stage premiere of the same composer's *Carmina Burana*. There was unanimous praise for the performance of Leontyne Price who sang the role of the wise maiden and for Lawrence Winters who was the king she married. It was Mr. Winter's debut role with the company. "I've done more than my share of dying on-stage," explained Leontyne later. She was delighted with the role because it gave her a chance to prove that "I'm a comedienne at heart."

Alfred Frankenstein, writing in the *San Francisco Chronicle* made the following comments: "Miss Price's voice is a little lighter in texture than those we are accustomed to hearing in this role. It has all the power the music demands, but it floats with a special quality that is new so far as *Aïda* is concerned, and is profoundly moving. But no singer, no matter how beautiful and individual the timbre of her voice, could have accomplished what Miss Price accomplished on vocal quality alone.

"Her ear is impeccable and so is her command of phrasing and nuance; over and above everything is her warm, vital, youthful and immensely appealing stage personality, which develops Aïda as a humanly heroic and completely believable character, without a trace of the prima donna in her makeup."

Miss Price had been scheduled to sing the name part in *Aïda* for the first time at the Vienna State Opera several months later. However, after Miss Stella was forced to cancel her engagement, San Franciscans were priviledged with being the first to hear her interpretation of the role.

On September 11, 1959, she was invited to open the thirty-seventh season of the San Francisco Opera Company with a performance of *Aïda*. Jon Vickers sang the role of Radames and Irene Dalis was cast as Amneris.

In 1960 an appendicitis operation in Vienna prevented Miss Price from arriving in time for the San Francisco Opera season. However, she sang *Madame Butterfly* when the opera company performed in Los Angeles. In 1961 she sang the role in San Francisco opposite Sandor Konya who was cast as Pinkerton.

In the fall of 1967 Miss Price returned to the scene of her first great onstage operatic triumph to head the cast of Verdi's *Un Ballo in Maschera* singing the role of Amelia. She celebrated the tenth anniversary of her professional operatic debut with the Company.

Miss Price refers to the San Francisco Opera Company as "my grand opera alma mater." When the audience applauded the lavish opening night performance of Verdi's *Ernani* on September 13, 1968, she sang the role of Elvira. It was the first time the work had been performed in San Francisco by that company, which signalled the 45th season of the house.

Heuwell Tircuit wrote of the brilliant performance in the *San Francisco Chronicle*: "For those who would rather hear the human larynx than an opera, there were a number of well trained ones in the cast. Leontyne Price brought her exceptional prowess to bear on the role of Elvira and did a really admirable job in this demanding part, so basically unsuitable to her voice. Good for her!

"The voice could not quite project itself in the ensemble numbers, but her solos, especially *Ernani, involami* (what a terrifying way to begin a role) and the duet *Ah, morir potessi adesso!* were electrifying."

In the *San Francisco Chronicle* Robert Commanday commented: "The role of Elvira, a hapless piece of femininity, hardly taxes Leontyne Price, but she only began taking good advantage of her few vocal opportunities in the second act. Before then, her singing was uneven, heavy and pushed in the low register and tending to lunge at the highs. The familiar grand warmth and vibrancy came on in Act II after a few thrilling high C sharps loosened her up."

The opulent opera audience included Regine Crespin and her husband, Lou Bruder; Grace Bumbry, Jon Vickers, Claramae Turner and Chester Ludgin.

At the last curtain call, the president of the Opera Association appeared onstage, and with the entire cast gathered around him, announced the establishment of the Kurt Herbert Adler Award—in honor of the man who introduced Leontyne Price to the American grand opera stage.

In 1958 during an interview with one of the San Francisco newspapers, Leontyne said that there were two roles she would someday like to sing. They were *Madame Butterfly* and *Louise*. She sang her first Butterfly at the Vienna Staatsoper in 1960. She has never sung the complete opera of *Louise* on stage; however she has recorded the aria *Depuis le jour* and has sung it in concert innumerable times.

THE CHICAGO LYRIC OPERA

Every season the Chicago Lyric Opera Company's productions contain a number of fresh voices. Very often they sing with the company before they have been heard at the Metropolitan. Leontyne Price, Birgit Nilsson, Eileen Farrell, and Leonie Rysanek all appeared with the Lyric before singing at the Met.

Leontyne Price first sang with the Chicago company the season before her historic debut at the Met. In the fall of 1959, she sang the lyric role of Liu in Puccini's *Turandot* for the Chicago Lyric Opera. She prefers the warm-hearted part to the icy title role. *Turandot* had been presented by the Lyric the preceding season. However, the casting of Miss Price as Liu added freshness making it one of the loveliest performances of the season.

Miss Price also sang *Thaïs* her first season at the Chicago Lyric Opera. However, it was a terrible fiasco. Larney Goodkind suggested her for the title role in the Massenet work. Carol Fox, general manager, loved the idea of casting Miss Price in the opera.

The critics thought she was unfortunately cast for the role. "As a courtesan," wrote Claudia Cassidy, "she is decorative and as a penitent she is demure. She has a lovely lyric voice of gleaming range, with the dusk in its shadows that sometimes finds the subtler meaning of French song. But she knows only the surface of the role, and she has been miserably coached. It is often hard to know what she is impersonating, unless it might be the Statue of Liberty."

In Roger Dettmer's commentary he stated: "It made no more sense to put Price in *Thaïs* than to star Tebaldi as Salome."

Leontyne Price is never defeated by things that haven't turned out the way she thinks they should. No matter how bad they may seem, she learns from them and puts forth a special effort to prevent a recurrence. She got some of her most caustic criticism after she sang *Thaïs*. Florence Page Kimball read them with her after warning her in advance that they were disappointing. Leontyne was very concerned about the results and asked her teacher:

"What do they say about my voice?"

"They say you have a wonderful, wonderful voice," her teacher assured her.

"All right then," she said quietly. "The rest I can learn and I will."

Every time Leontyne went to Chicago for performances at the Lyric Opera, she was greeted by Danny Newman, publicity director, who was accompanied by photographers.

Danny always presented her with the rehearsal schedule and escorted her to the hotel where she would be residing.

He had met Miss Price back in 1952 and handled the tour of *Porgy and Bess* prior to the European engagements. In fact, he was the one who had announced to William Warfield that she had been selected to sing the role of Bess with him.

Mr. Newman found her voice very exciting and wanted to hear every performance she did after he first heard her. "She is a fine artist—gifted, serious, and is a very magnetic stage personality—and a very beautiful woman," he said.

When Leontyne first arrived in Chicago, Danny remembered that in 1953 she and Bill presented him with a wallet when he was leaving the *Porgy and Bess* Company for a new position in Buenos Aires, Argentina.

John Peters, master of wardrobe of the Lyric, went to Leontyne's hotel on Thanksgiving Day to fit her for costumes when she sang the lead role in *Madame Butterfly*. She did not have her own costumes. Mr. Peters was accompanied by Christopher West.

Miss Price did not appear to feel secure her first years in Chicago. She was quite concerned about how she would come across to the audience visually. She wanted to wear a wig because she felt that it would make her look more oriental for the role of Cio-Cio-San.

"I want it to come off right; I owe so much of my career to Miss Fox," she told John Peters.

Leontyne wanted everyone to be pleased with her because she was doing everything for others. She cared so much for her music and wanted to leave the details to someone else.

When she sang the part of Aïda she had brought along her own costumes. One dress which was made of jersey fabric did not fit properly across the bust. No one had suggested an alteration to her before. But John Peters pointed it out and corrected it by making a cleavage which made her very pleased.

John had heard Price perform back in Dallas, Texas, and thought she was wonderful. At the time she had not become famous, but he recognized that she had great talent. He had no idea that she would some day be singing grand opera. "I thought her career was set for *Porgy and Bess* the rest of her life," he said.

G. Richard Ryan, production assistant at the Lyric, was pleased to work with Leontyne Price. When he first encountered her he did not know what to expect. "I was literally delighted and surprised to see how down to earth she was." Ryan stated that many American singers who have gone abroad return to the United States with a foreign accent. "But Price was just plain and down to earth," he added. "She was a dream to get along with and was always thankful for everything anyone did for her."

During the staging of *Aïda* when the slaves are parading by during the Triumphal March, Leontyne had small parts to sing. Ryan became disturbed because she had to stand for such a long period of time. He found a stool for her to sit on.

"Oh, that's marvelous," she said. She sat down, but only for about thirty seconds. "I just can't do it." She couldn't remain seated while her colleagues were at work.

Dick Ryan was standing at stage right during the actual performance of *Aïda*. "I was amazed at her strength—both physical and emotional. Her voice soared effortlessly over the top of the orchestra".

"During her last performance of *Aïda*, a fly tried to land on her forehead while she was singing. She did everything possible to shoo him away without distracting the audience. She sang beautifully while the whole backstage crew seemed riveted," said Ryan.

CHAPTER VI

PERFORMING ABROAD

It is a common characteristic for most American opera singers to go to Europe in search of a career; but for Leontyne Price, the foundation was carefully laid months before her grand opera debut on the Continent. André Mertens, anxious to promote his protégé, seized every possible opportunity to expose her to individuals he thought would be beneficial in launching her career.

After seeing Leontyne appear in *Porgy and Bess* in 1953, he became her concert manager. As Executive Vice President and as Director of Columbia Artists Management, Inc., he obviously was in a position to book her immediately and effectively. It was logical enough that he should take an interest in her; for he was already the manager of William Warfield. Mertens had been a manager since 1923 and once served in the Ministry of Fine Arts in the pre-Hitlerian German government. He always prided himself as being one capable of spotting talent.

Speaking of his first time hearing Miss Price, Mertens said: "I saw immediately in her the potential. I got her concerts right away and she did a helluva lot of them." Mertens believed that his own major contribution to Leontyne's career was bringing her together with von Karajan whom he had known since 1929. "It was not a difficult chore for me," said Mertens. "She always had a great flair and she was a thorough musician."

In 1955, Mertens took Leontyne to Carnegie Hall for an audition. Arriving with her accompanist, she had no idea who was going to hear her. As she began to sing an aria from *Aïda*, she noticed a slim good-looking gentleman seated in the aisle, casually eating a club sandwich. His black hair, flecked with gray, added to his continental appearance. Leontyne, singing with a sophisticated technique, astonished her listener. Before she ended the last note, the distinguished auditor stopped eating and abandoned his sandwich. Rushing to the piano, he excitedly pushed the accompanist aside and began to play for her himself. She sang "Pace, pace, mio dio!" from *La Forza del Destino*, even more convincingly.

"My God! I'm getting goose pimples," he said, startled at what he had just heard.

After her second aria, Leontyne learned that she had sung for Herbert von Karajan, conductor of the Vienna Symphony Orchestra. Karajan was at Carnegie Hall rehearsing for his first concert in the United States. Mertens had brought him to America as musical director and conductor of the Berlin Philharmonic Orchestra. Mertens felt that Leontyne would be one of the greatest artists of the time. Consequently, as a personal favor, he had persuaded the maestro to interrupt his busy schedule to hear her.

It had been Mertens' aim from the outset to give Leontyne as much international exposure as possible before she made her debut at the Metropolitan. He wanted her to have experience and repertoire at her command. This would give her the needed self-confidence for a successful entrée into the Met.

It is necessary for American opera singers to be well prepared for the operatic world. In Europe there are numerous opera companies where singers are taught their roles and are privileged with rehearsals. Companies of this kind are very limited in the United States, but at the same time, American singers are required to know their roles when they arrive abroad. Usually, before the actual performance, there is only a short staging rehearsal at which time singers are told to go in a certain direction.

Von Karajan was deeply impressed with Leontyne's

artistic ability. A man of great vision and acumen, he did not waste any time exposing his new operatic prodigy to the European musical world. As soon as he returned to Vienna, he began to lay the groundwork for her operatic debut on his side of the Atlantic.

He invited her to sing the role of *Salome* at La Scala, Milan's famed opera house. Having never sung the role, she was in no hurry to tackle it. After consulting with Mertens and her other advisors, she responded negatively. They had concluded that she was not ready for the part. Von Karajan, therefore, was informed that she wanted to wait a couple of years until she had properly learned it. However, she did sing *Aïda* with him at the Vienna Staatsoper in 1958. Her performance was so successful that even the members of the orchestra, who were generally very conservative with their applause, stood up to give her a genuine ovation.

Singing with Herbert von Karajan so early in her operatic career was almost like starting at the top. The conductor has a stature that very few musicians have in Europe. He is often referred to as the "General Musik Director of Europe." That performance of *Aïda*, therefore skyrocketed Leontype Price into international fame.

Mertens flew to Vienna to be with Leontyne when she sang *Aïda*. He said later: "Wor me, who left Germany right after Hitler came to power, it was the crowning point of my career, that in Vienna, where National Socialism more or less started, this American Negro girl was treated with the greatest deference by everybody, just like a queen."

Von Karajan liked her interpretation of *Aïda* and kept inviting her to come back to Vienna. The following season she was engaged to sing her first Pamina in the *Magic Flute*. German had always been a problem for her since her first class in that language back at Wilberforce. Her southern accent came across very strongly during the performance. Eric Kunz who sang the role of Vogelfanger, the birdcatcher, remarked in jest: "I just won't do **The Magic Flute** with you any more, Leontyne, because you are getting all the laughs. Pamina isn't supposed to get any laughs." However, the reviews by the Vienna press were favorable. Leontyne was not panned because of the flaws in her German singing. The press stated that the role of Pamina had not been sung that way for many years.

Miss Price made her operatic debut at the Royal Opera House, Covent Garden, winning one of the most overwhelming acclamations received by an American opera singer in Europe. Cast as Aïda on the evening of July 2, 1958, she paired with Regina Resnik in the leading feminine roles. Miss Resnik, Metropolitan Opera mezzo-soprano, sang the part of Amneris.

There were sporadic cheers throughout the evening and the audience kept shouting and applauding long after the lights had gone up at the end of the performance. Both singers wept at the reception and at the outburst of bravos that greeted Miss Resnik's kiss for Miss Price when they took a final bow together.

Leontyne had already made an indelible mark on Londoners. Reminiscent were the days when she sang the part of Bess at London's Stoll Theater several years earlier. However, that role was a completely different type of sensation. In addition, her singing *Aïda* was a dramatic step forward vocally.

"There are more than a thousand miles and more than a few years between the Stoll Theater and the Royal Opera House," Miss Price said. "This is something special and it means that work I did since 1952 was well worthwhile.... It's like being on Cloud 16. It was overwhelming, physically as well as emotionally, for me when the audience accepted me so well."

While in London to sing *Aïda*, Miss Price took time out to display her talents to a vast home audience of radio listeners and television viewers. Her first radio broadcast was on May 27, 1959. She skillfully sang Helena's Aria from Richard Strauss's *Die Aegyptische Helena*. She was ably supported by the British Broadcasting Corporation Symphony Orchestra which was conducted by Peter Herman Adler. The following week on June 4th, the English got a good look at her as well as listening satisfaction when she gave a television recital accompanied by Gerald Moore. Mr. Moore played for her again on July 4th for her recital of American Songs.

That same year she made a tour of Yugoslavia and did recitals at the Brussels World's Fair. She also was in a concert of the Verdi *Requiem* in the Musikverein.

Shirley Verrett sang in a performance of Verdi's *Requiem* with Leontyne Price at La Scala. Due to a mix-up in the scheduling, Miss Verrett was not able to have an orchestral rehearsal with Herbert von Karajan. Leontyne was extremely exhausted because she had been involved in the making of a film. However, she approached Miss Verrett saying: "Shirley, I'll go over this afternoon and sing the 'Agnus Dei'."

This is a very difficult aria because in that particular part the voices are two octaves apart.

"No," said Shirley. "You should be resting. Don't come just for me. We'll do all right. I know what you're going to do. We'll work together."

"Oh, no, Sweetie," said Leontyne. "I have got to go over there and sing that with you."

Shirley was really touched by Leontyne's kind consideration because she knew how tired she was. When the two ladies appeared for the rehearsal, the pianist at La Scala remarked: "I've never seen this done. Very, very rarely will one singer help another like this when she is tired."

Miss Price always gets some of her best audience response in Washington, D. C., Vienna and San Francisco. "I always feel I've halfway won before I finish," she said. When she made her opera debut in Paris on February 2, 1968, the audience jeered the ballet, conductor, orchestra, staging, decor, spear carriers and the costumes. However, the same audience was warm to Leontyne and was enthusiastic about her performance. Appearing as Aïda, her interpretation of "*O patria mia*" stopped the show for more than two minutes.

Maria Callas was so impressed with Miss Price's performance that she invited the diva to supper for just the two of them.

The Baroness Elie de Rothschild, affectionately known as Liliane, gave a luncheon in honor of Miss Price in her *Grande Salle à Manger* on February 9. Her slender mustachioed husband is at the top of one of the greatest international banking fortunes. An avid admirer of Miss Price, the svelte baroness served Pintade Limousine with string beans as her main course. In addition to Miss Price, some of the other guests included Mademoiselle Cecile de Rothschild, Monsieur Douglas Cooper, Monsieur Francois Valery and Monsieur Herve Mille. Chateau du Chatelard 1966 and Chateau Lafits-Rothschild 1947 were the selected wines for the occasion.

Leontyne Price made her first appearance in Moscow as one of the singers of Verdi's *Requiem* in the fall of 1964. She appeared with La Scala as part of a giant cultural exchange between Italy and the Soviet Union. Performing with Miss Price were Birgit Nilsson and Joan Sutherland.

On the first night Leontyne was suffering from bronchitis. After the performance she was unhappy with the way she had sung. However, she was encouraged tremendously by the enthusiastic reception of the Bolshoi Opera House audience. Miss Price and the other singers were called back for sixteen bows over twenty-six minutes.

It was a "sensational audience to sing to—I would easily like to come back," said an ailing Miss Price. "This is sort of like Vienna, the same amount of applause we get there," she added.

A large number of autograph seekers mobbed Miss Price as she was leaving the theater. The United States Embassy cultural attaché and Miss Price's manager had to fight their way through the crowd to the attaché's automobile. It was reported that Miss Price looked frightened and was on the verge of panic.

On the morning of the second performance, Miss Price's condition had not improved. She was coughing and was not in her best form. However, she had been "extremely emotional about this occasion."

The soprano stated, "The warmth of the audience was most incredible. It contradicts what I see out of my hotel window: a sort of regimented life, people lining up on the streets to buy things.

"This was completely undisciplined here—it was sort of mad and fun for me, an experience I wouldn't have missed for the world."

Although Leontyne loathed the German language heartily, she has astounded many of her friends of longstanding that she got along so well in Vienna and with von Karajan, a native German. In the summer of 1959 she had a very successful interview by a number of Viennese journalists in the Franz Lehar Room of the Ambassador Hotel. Seated at a table close by were George Jellinek, his wife and daughter. The journalists were successful in interviewing Miss Price part in English and part in German. At that time she had gone to Vienna to sing at the Staatsoper. In referring to her efforts to express herself in that language, Leontyne recalls "how wretched the German was."

Leontyne Price was scheduled to sing in the Luchino Visconti production of *Il Trovatore* in Vienna. However, her appearance was interrupted because of an appendectomy. She was touched when she got a phone call from her husband, Bill Warfield. Gwyneth Jones could hardly believe it when informed that she would replace the ailing Miss Price as Leonora. She had never dreamed she would be offered the role and it had to be repeated to the startled young soprano three times before she could believe it.

"I was quite thrilled and rather surprised, to put it mildly," said Miss Jones, "when they told me I was going to replace Leontyne Price for all the performances."

Leontyne had walked many times through Milan's famous Piazza della Scala, past the ornate brown-brick theater with the triple-arched main entrance. It is considered the number one opera house in Italy, but she had never been inside the theater. "I swore," she said, "that I would not enter as a tourist until I sang there."

On May 21, 1960, her long-awaited dream became reality. She walked through the stage door of La Scala to make a triumphant debut. Cast as Aïda, she appeared without a single stage rehearsal. "After all," she said, "what's the problem? The Nile can only be upstage." She was the first black singer to appear in a major part in an Italian opera at La Scala.

In Italy claques are organized to make all kinds of noise to give a great impression on the singer. An artist, therefore, does not know the real effect he has on the audience. These hired groups are usually seated in the eaves during the performance. In many instances they lead off the audience with applause that is meaningless. The singers must pay the claque or they will get boos from them instead of cheers. At La Scala, especially, singers appearing stand in awe of the claque. When Leontyne made her debut, she decided that if she had to engage the claque, she would pay them to shut up and not applaud. A confident Miss Price knew she was going to be a success and, therefore, wanted to stand on her own merit and see how she would come across with the audience.

Aïda had been performed six times at La Scala during that season, but every seat was occupied that night. Leontyne came across with great success taking curtain calls repeatedly after each act. In addition to crying out "Brava, Brava," some of the opera lovers even made yells of "Divina," a term of enthusiasm that is usually reserved for La Scala's veteran singers.

A critic of Milan's *Corriere Della Sera* said, "Her voice is firm and assured. She is splendid and sweet in the high register .... she has very fine phrasing. Besides the technical side, her best quality is the happy intense power of expression which permits her to give her singing the exact tone suitable for Verdi's opera."

Miss Price manipulated her big soprano voice with conviction and faultless accuracy. Her interpretation of *Aïda* was feline and tender as well as sweet and aggressive. She won bravos after her opening trio with Radames and Amneris. This place in the opera had not drawn cheers at La Scala in many years. She got many more ovations as she ranged effortlessly from finespun pianissimos to magnificently ringing fortes. "Brava, Leonessa!" cried someone in the audience. A second voice retorted, "She is more like a panther than a lioness."

One critic commented, "Our great Verdi would have found her the ideal Aïda." Another critic regretted that Miss Price's race might bar her from appearing in other roles. However, a La Scala official promised that there would be no color problem and added, "The public will have to get used to it. If she sings Butterfly and anybody objects, we'll say she's a suntanned Butterfly."

Later, when Leontyne was engaged to sing *Madame Butterfly* at La Scala, she scored a new triumph. The spectators were somewhat puzzled at first seeing the black singer in the role of the fragile Japanese girl Cio-Cio-San. It was the first time a woman of color had performed in *Madame Butterfly* at La Scala. She received many curtain calls after each act and an ovation at the end of the performance. Although the production had already been performed by other artists fourteen times that year, Miss Price's name was sufficient to draw a sellout audience.

Salzburg, long noted for its performances of the works of Wolfgang Amadeus Mozart, had an added attraction when it presented its unusually brilliant *Don Giovanni* in the summer of 1960. It had as its leading protagonist on the distaff side, Leontyne Price. "For the first time within memory of most Salzburgers, Donna Anna managed the dramatic fire of '*Or sai chi l'onore*,' as well as the coloratura of '*Non mir dir,*'" wrote Martin Bernheimer in the *New York Herald Tribune*. "Furthermore," he continued, "she could act with equal mobility and passion, and had perfect control of both Mozart's style and her own vocal equipment."

Fresh from triumphs in San Francisco, Chicago, La Scala, Covent Garden and a variety of other opera houses on the Continent, Miss Price's background was at variance with those of most of the *Don Giovanni* cast. She had successfully made the big switch from Broadway to grand opera. Unlike most of her colleagues, she was not a leading singer in one of the major German opera houses.

One critic said that in that production von Karajan took the larghetto of Donna Anna's second aria as if it were allegretto, and the allegretto as if it were marked larghetto. Miss Price, however, gave her stamp of approval to von Karajan's eccentricity. She also sang it beautifully and convincingly. "I felt it that way too," she asserted.

In speaking about the maestro Miss Price said: "I think he is an extremely aware conductor—vocally. I always had an enormous amount of easiness and fun singing with him from a vocal point of view. There is an incredible rapport."

"Von Karajan had this big, fat, crackpot idea of my doing Donna Anna in Salzburg," Price commented later in jest. However, she performed the role and did exactly the way he wanted her to do it. Claudia Cassidy, the Chicago critic, did not like the unusual interpretation of part of the opera. "Von Karajan made her a tiger cat," she said. "No one had ever done the role like that before."

It was after she sang Donna Anna in Salzburg that Leontyne Price was properly invited to the Metropolitan. That was when she was offered a decent contact . . . . It was in 1960. When she got her first offer from the Met prior to that, she promptly turned it down. It was decided that it was the wrong contract and the wrong time. In fact, at that time she was doing something else.

With Herbert von Karajan conducting the Vienna Philharmonic Orchestra, Leontyne Price, Giulietta Simionato, Franco Corelli and Ettore Bastianini were engaged for performances of *Il Trovatore*. The vocally resplendent cast convened for the 1962 summer season of the Salzburg Festival. The performance was really extraordinary. Tickets for that performance were the most difficult to obtain in Europe. The few that could be found sold for forty dollars each.

Commenting later about the opera Miss Price stated: "There was a performance of *Il Trovatore* in Salzburg with Corelli, Bastianini, Simionato and myself which was just Not to Be Believed! Everyone was great and you felt that there were seventeen voices instead of four. On that kind of night, when you give it all you've got and even you feel this was it and say to yourself 'find me somebody who can do this better,' well, there's no touching you with a twenty-foot pole for at least a day. It's un-be-lievably exciting."

Credit Cecil Thompson

Leontyne Price as Amelia in *Un Ballo in Maschera*, 1965. Sandor Konya on the left; Raymond Wolansky on the right. San Francisco Memorial Opera House.

Credit Cecil Thompson
Leontyne Price as Tosca, 1963. San Francisco Memorial Opera House.

WAR MEMORIAL OPERA HOUSE
San Francisco Press Dept.

Leontyne Price receiving the Honorary Degree of Doctor of Music at Fordham University, Bronx, N. Y.

Photo by Publicity Dept., Lyric Opera
Leontyne Price and Michael Roux in *Thaïs,* 1959. Lyric Opera of Chicago.

Credit Farabola, Milan

Leontyne Price arriving in Milan, Italy, for performances at La Scala, 1962.

Photo by Metropolitan Opera House Press Dept.

LINCOLN CENTER FOR THE PERFORMING ARTS. Metropolitan Opera House in the Center.

Photo by Publicity Dept., Lyric Opera

Leontyne Price arriving in Chicago for performances at the Lyric Opera.

Leontyne Price as Minnie in *Girl of the Golden West*. Metropolitan Opera House.

Credit Louis Melancon

Credit Louis Melancon
Leontyne Price as Fiordiligi in *Cosi Fan Tutte*. Metropolitan Opera House.

Leontyne Price as Cleopatra in *Antony and Cleopatra*. Metropolitan Opera House.

Credit Louis Melancon

Credit Louis Melancon

Leontyne Price as Aïda. Metropolitan Opera House.

Hugh Lee Lyon

Leontyne Price:
Highlights of a Prima Donna

CHAPTER VII

OLD METROPOLITAN OPERA HOUSE

When Leontyne Price arrived at the Metropolitan Opera House she was thoroughly prepared. She was fortunate in having good advisers and excellent management. She arrived as an international singer with experience and a repertoire at her command. The confident Miss Price had refused to accept an earlier engagement. "I felt I wasn't ready," she stated candidly.

Opera fans had eagerly awaited her debut for several years. This fact explains the electric atmosphere in the house the night the thirty-four-year-old soprano appeared on the tradition-filled stage for the first time. She sang the role of Leonora in *Il Trovatore* on January 27, 1961.

Arriving just at the right time in her career, she had already done well on the operatic stage because of her varied experiences. In addition to singing in Laurel during her pre-college days and at Wilberforce College, she had sung at concerts in a variety of cities, at festivals, Town Hall, San Francisco, India, Australia, Vienna, London, La Scala and over television networks. A seasoned artist, she didn't have to work her way up through the ranks as many singers do.

Leontyne really grew during her first four years of grand opera. To begin with, she received a good vocal technique from her teacher. She was able to let her voice grow properly. She, therefore, was prepared for the great distances one has to go in opera. However, the quality of her voice had not changed.

Leontyne is always eager to learn and takes advice

willingly. Florence Page Kimball went to the rehearsal of *Il Trovatore* at the Metropolitan. She sat there with her notebook and jotted down suggestions for improvement. Later at Longchamps Restaurant she said, "Leontyne, it was lovely. If I don't read you one of these notes, you will still give a magnificent performance."

She insisted on hearing every one of her teacher's comments. Miss Kimball explained to her that in one place she went up the scale too heavily and that the attack should have been freer on the first high C. The morning of the performance she called her teacher and said she felt completely confident. She also mentioned that she was carefully thinking over the suggestions.

She floated onstage to sing the dazzling part of Leonora, the Spanish noblewoman. Her first aria, the dulcet *"Tacea la notte placida"* (Calm is the Night), served notice to her listeners that she had already carved an indelible place in operatic annals.

Franco Corelli, the tenor who sang the role of Manrico, was dressed in a velvet tunic which displayed his legs—his most famous physical asset. They have earned him the Milan nickname of "Golden Calves."

"I just love Franco," says Leontyne Price. "He has such gorgeous legs."

Leontyne did everything her teacher had suggested to her after the rehearsal. When she sang the last aria of the opera, she received one of the most remarkable demonstrations ever to greet a Metropolitan Opera debut. For forty-two minutes after the great gold curtain descended, cheers and cries of "Price! Price!" resounded through the Manhattan hall.

"I was in the theatre the night she made her debut," said Martina Arroyo. "And God, was that a night! You didn't believe those sounds were coming out of a human being. It was just so beautiful. That was an exciting night altogether. Mr. Corelli was making his debut and Robert Merrill was in excellent voice. It was just unbelievable."

Due to concert engagements, Bill Warfield was not present when his wife made her debut, but he sent her a telegram and flowers. However, the big triumph was shared by Leontyne's parents and the Chisholm family. The Prices sat in the 10th row orchestra seats. Nearby were Mr. and Mrs. Chisholm and all three of their daughters.

"I'm very happy," said Mrs. Price. "My work has been accomplished."

Mr. Chisholm added, "It's like betting on a horse and watching it win."

At that time Shirley Verrett was a voice student at Juilliard with Madame Freschl. Shirley and one of her girl friends were present for Leontyne's debut. That night they sat at one of the score desks. Shirley didn't have enough money to buy a seat in the orchestra. However, Juilliard students could pay one dollar for a score desk. They could easily leave the desk to go for a good glimpse of the performance.

Shirley sat on the edge of one of the tables, possibly blocking the view of someone else. She was absolutely thrilled by what she was hearing. "Many people get all kinds of reactions when they hear a great singer, but rarely does a singer give me goosepimples," said Shirley, "but I sat there all night rubbing my arms."

After the performance, still fresh and stunning from her first Met triumph, Leontyne encountered Rudolf Bing backstage. He asked how she was doing. "Mr. Bing," she said excitedly, "I'm having a ball."

The Chisholms gave a party in her honor at the Biltmore Hotel later that night. After having sung the enormous role of Leonora, Leontyne arrived for the reception about two o'clock. She warmly greeted the countless guests and one of them requested that she sing something for them.

"Nobody's going to leave this party unhappy," she said.

She walked to the middle of the room and enchanted her guests with "Summertime."

Before her debut, Miss Price had told a reporter: "I am

terribly excited, but not nervous. I am thrilled to sing at the Metropolitan, which I consider to be an extraordinary opera house, possibly the greatest in the world."

Her debut season was one of the heaviest and most exciting single schedules ever shouldered by a newcomer. Larney Goodkind had advised her astutely and she had stayed out of the Met until she was throughly prepared. "Look, Leontyne," said Goodkind pleading with her, "they've been hearing all these exciting reports about you and maybe Bing has even sneaked into certain places where you were singing and has actually heard you. I am sure he has. Naturally the Met is your goal, but don't go there now.

"Whenever you get to the Met," he continued, "don't ever make the mistake of singing a role for the first time in your life at the Met. Only sing roles there after you've done them elsewhere and proven them to yourself and everybody else. When you go to the Met you've got to go there with solidly learned roles down cold under your belt . . . a good number of them. You've got engagements for all kinds of roles ahead at the Vienna Staatsoper, Covent Garden, the San Francisco Opera, the Chicago. Those are your opportunities to do roles and try them out—be sure they are right for you and that you like them."

Leontyne followed Mr. Goodkind's advice and in the succeeding years she got five good solid roles that were a part of her. She had a fantastic debut season. In nine weeks time she did all five of them and just laid them in the aisles just one right after the other. In addition to Leonora in *Il Trovatore*, she sang the title role in *Aïda*, Donna Anna in Mozart's *Don Giovanno*, Cio-Cio-San in Puccini's *Madama Butterfly* and Liu in *Turandot*.

"I am really quite secure artistically since I have performed all five roles before and can sing them better now," said Miss Price.

Bill has seen every opera in which his wife has performed. Aida, however, was the first role he heard her sing *Aïda* at the Metropolitan. Although he was not in town for her debut in *Trovatore*, he heard her sing a repeat performance of that opera later. Bill Warfield flew in from California to hear his wife perform at the Metropolitan for the first time. Seated about ten rows from the stage, he observed her beautifully workout creation of the role.

Costumed in a flowing white gown, adorned with gold and pearls, Miss Price camem across as a statusque *Aïda*. Due to her dramatic ability and sensitivity to the African motif, she was described by patrons as the most impressive *Aïda* they had seen in many years. An enormous chorus of black singers led by Eugene Brice represented the slaves with youthful black dancers from the Mary Bruce School in Harlem.

The New York Times' highly respected Ross Parmenter was unstinted in his praise and made the following commentary:

"The glory of her performance was its singing, but its excellence in other respects should not go unnoticed.

"Let those other virtues be spoken of first. For a start, there was a splendid physical appearance.

"She was an Aïda of such physical attractiveness that, for once, it was thoroughly understandable that Radames should prefer her to the high-born princess.

"Then there was Miss Price's acting. Perhaps in later performances it will grow a little more subtle in the first acts, but it is already a beautifully worked-out creation.

"One touch, perhaps, will illustrate its intelligence, its grace and its expressiveness.

"It occurred in the second act. By this time it was abundantly clear that Aida deeply loved Radames.

"And when Radames freed his prisoners, including Aïda's father, Miss Price looked at him with such suddenly heightened adoration that her grief at the end of the scene as he was turned over to Amneris was utterly convincing."

Richard Wagner, Charles Gounod and Gioacchino Rossini considered *Don Giovanni* one of the greatest operas ever composed. Leontyne Price got ravishing reviews when she sang it at the Met the first time. A review by the New *York Times* on March 27, 1961, mentioned that "Leontyne Price sang the part of Donna Anna for the first time here, and the soprano's much anticipated performance proved well worth waiting for. Indeed, this reviewer thinks it unlikely that the Metropolitan has had any Donna Anna to compare with Miss Price during the last decade, at least."

In addition to the dramatic role of Donna Anna, Miss Price has also sung the lighter part of Donna Elvira in *Don Giovanni*. She feels that Donna Elvira stands closer to her emotionally. "She is definitely the better character, in my personal opinion," said Miss Price. "She's feminine; everything about her is extremely real," she added. However, Miss Price feels that her vocal gifts match closer to Donna Anna although the latter character is aloof—more detached.

On the night of October 23, 1961, she became the first Negro to have the honor of opening a Metropolitan Opera season. The honor of opening the opera season is one coveted by prima donnas. She sang the role of Minnie in a new production of Puccini's *The Girl of the Golden West*. This was the first time this opera had been presented at the Met in thirty years. Her career reached its peak as she sang the part of the tender-hearted barmaid of the Last Chance Saloon.

A musicians' dispute threatened to cancel the Metropolitan Opera season that year. However, Arthur Goldberg, Secretary of Labor, intervened and a settlement was made in time for opening night.

"The Metropolitan is a national institution and it just had to go on," said the soprano backstage.

Although he did not attend the performance, President John F. Kennedy was in complete agreement with Miss Price. "The entire nation rejoices that this distinguished cultural asset to our national life will again bring the special performances of great artists to millions of American homes," he said in a congratulatory telegram to Secretary Goldberg.

Irving Kolodin made the following comments on *The Girl of the Golden West* which is known in Italy as *La Fanciulla del West*:

"She took in her stride the challenge posed by this opening night assignment in a role she had never sung publicly before, as well as the burden of being the first prima donna of her race to earn such an opportunity. The natural assumption that her voice will grow in size with use was borne out by the power she summoned at will: but there was also the sensitive command of nuance to make the quieter moments of Acts I and II count for the contrast the composer planned. Lacking, however, was a physical illusion of the *viso d'angelo* (face of an angel) praised by her bandit-lover. These are hard facts to face for an artist of Miss Price's quality; but they must be reckoned with if she is to make the most of her abilities."

On a night during November, 1961, a pall fell over the Metropolitan Opera House. Leontyne was on the stage singing in another performance of *Girl of the Golden West*.

Dorothy Kirsten, her understudy, had been given the signal to retire for the night. She had taken her sleeping pills and was cozily sleeping in her New York City hotel room. Leontyne, having made a successful appearance in Act I, returned to the stage for the second act. Toward the end of Act II, something went wrong. Her vocal instrument, laden with feeling and warmth, began to get weaker and weaker. Suddenly the bejeweled voice had absented itself completely from the throat of the soprano who stood at the pinnacle of the operatic world.

Dorothy Kirsten was the only soprano available who could sing the part. She had to be awakened and was called in to replace a troubled colleague. It was later announced that Leontyne's voice had failed her due to a serious virus infection.

George Shirley who was present that night stated: "I heard her when she lost her voice. It definitely was the most traumatic moment of her life. She was certainly brave to try to finish the opera, but she was in vocal trouble and the voice just sort of disappeared. It led to her having to take time off to repair and then build for her comeback.

"*Fanciulla* certainly was a great plum for her. It was only unfortunately after she became involved in it, she found out that it wasn't her meat necessarily. It's a different kind of role, different weight, a different demand all the way around.

"The audience was a bit uncomfortable as the voice began slowly to disappear." George continued. "Everyone was wishing and I was wishing, too, that she would just stop. But she wouldn't do that. And I can appreciate her not wanting to bring the performance to a halt. But everybody was very uncomfortable about it because they realized what was happening."

Miss Price recalls her personal feelings at that time, "When I started to speak the words, I was forced to add something in place of song. This time there was an accent and a meaning to the words that I never had before, and the card game was more exciting than ever. Naturally, I prefer to sing the role, but it was an experience from which I learned a great deal."

She had received a wire saying the opening had been called off because of the impending musicians' strike, so she immediately went flying off to enjoy herself. Halfway through her vacation, she was told to report to New York and, consequently, began the season in a very fatigued state. This eventually affected her in a drastic manner. However, she says that good things come from crises because it was at that time that she really fell in love with Rome.

In November, 1961, Miss Price informed Larney Goodkind, her manager of nine years, that she wanted to sever her relationship with him. There had been an increase in tension between the two of them for quite some time. Mr. Goodkind, although shocked by her action, was not completely surprised.

"Why? What's the trouble?" he asked her.

"I just want that," she answered.

"After all that's taken place, the way we've worked together and what's happened with your career; the point it has reached. I consider I did a most successful job," said Larney.

"Well, I think I could have done it all on my own without you," Miss Price retorted.

Mr. Goodkind served papers on Miss Price in the Supreme Court of New York State alleging that she had breached an agreement between them and had fired him. She, in turn, countersued and filed a motion in the Supreme Court seeking dismissal of this complaint. The case never went to trial because a settlement was made between the two parties.

Leontyne had met Hubert Dilworth when both were appearing in *Porgy and Bess*. They became very good friends and he was of invaluable assistance to her. When they were in Europe he would get things done for her because of his foreign language facility. He would also act as her escort to many places. He began to function as her secretary. After she split up with Larney Goodkind, Dilworth became her personal manager also. He loves her art and her talent. He has become very devoted to her. At times he is a whipping boy and other times Leontyne deifies him.

When Tchaikovsky's *Eugene Onegin* returned to the Metropolitan during the eighteenth week of the 1963-64 season, Leontyne Price led the newcomers in the role of Tatyana. With Thomas Schippers conducting the work for the first time, William Dooley made his debut with the Metropolitan in the title role.

On January 3, 1964, Leontyne Price sang her first Pamina in the *Magic Flute* with the Metropolitan Opera Company. That season, along with two new singers, she sang in the fifth performance. John Alexander sang the role of Tamino and David Ward made his debut at the Met as Sarastro. William Walker who had already sung Papageno that season added greatly to the stability of the performance.

Mr. Bing had asked Mr. Walker to sing the role during the baritone's second season at the Metropolitan. He was a young kid that almost nobody had heard of. Bill first heard Leontyne's voice when he was in the summer stock chorus in Pittsburgh in the early nineteen fifties. There were some preliminary trials of a road company of *Porgy and Bess*. Bill Walker, along with the whole summer stock chorus, was invited to a dress rehearsal of the show. "I remember being completely overwhelmed by the opulent beauty of her voice and the force of her personality on stage," said Bill. All the chorus was invited to a supper party given for the cast in Pittsburgh's Hill District. The exciting Leontyne already had an adoring throng of followers.

When Bill reported for rehearsals for the *Magic Flute* present were Leontyne Price, Cesare Siepi, Nicolai Gedda, Roberta Peters and many other luminaries from the operatic world. Up until that point Bill had sung the roles of jailers, commissaries and various and sundry small parts. This was his novel opportunity to sing in the operatic big leagues. He approached the first rehearsal at the Old Met with fear and trepidation. The star-studded cast went up on the roof stage which was on the top floor in the back of the house. It was a great barn-like place. As Bill Walker walked in, the first person he spotted was Leontyne Price "all swathed in leopard and a beautiful Cardin suit or something similar." Cesare was well groomed and debonair with his traditional continental air. Roberta was gorgeously coiffed and dressed.

There was a certain amount of camaraderie between the famous artists. Suddenly Bill realized what it was like being in the big league with the famous singers. He went over in a corner and sat down by himself. He stayed out of it completely until the conductor entered. He asked that the artists proceed with the scene between Pamina and Papageno where Miss Price and Bill Walker would sing together.

"Who is Papageno?" the conductor inquired.

Bill stood up and said, "I am."

"Who are you?" he asked.

"I am William Walker," the young singer responded.

Bill went over to Leontyne and said, "Excuse me, Miss Price, but I'm Bill Walker."

Leontyne turned to him and said: "Lord, Honey, I know you. You have been on the television. I see you all the time."

"Well, thank you," said Bill.

"Let's begin our scene," Leontyne suggested.

The scene opened and Pamina was seated on a great square cushion in the middle of the stage. Papageno went on to the scene and his first line in the English translation is "Oh, maiden young and fair, much whiter than a pigeon." This was the line that Bill was going to sing to her. He, very nervous, had certain misgivings about singing that line to Leontyne. "If she takes exception to it, I'll just have to live with it because that's what the translation says; and I'm not going to be able to change anything at this point, particularly in this rehearsal," Bill said to himself.

He walked up in full face and sang to Pamina: "Oh, maiden young and fair, much whiter than a pigeon." They finished the whole scene and there was a break.

"Bill, Honey!" Leontyne said to him. "Come here a minute, will you please?"

He went over to her and said, "Yes?"

"You know that first line about 'much whiter than a pigeon.'"

"Yes, I do," Bill answered.

"You know, I think maybe you'd better change that to much fairer than a pigeon because this pigeon ain't never been white."

Bill, completely flabbergasted by Leontyne's remark, burst into laughter. She was such an angel about it. He and Leontyne have been great friends ever since that first rehearsal.

The English dialogue between Bill and Leontyne was really amusing. Bill's West Texas twang and Leontyne with the "honey in her mouth" from Mississippi made a droll combination on stage. The English translation in the scene between the two of them was in complete shambles. Musically, it was superb, but it was a complete disaster as far as dialogue was concerned. Bill Walker's wife remembers that she could understand the prompter much better than she could Leontyne or her husband.

Miles Kastendieck noted that "Miss Price's first Pamina had that purity and beauty of voice expected of her. Her natural simplicity and artistry served her dependably. She made an appealing heroine without yet achieving quite the vocal distinction another performance should bring."

Theodore Strongin, writing in the *New York Times*, commented: "Miss Price, true musician that she is, sang with utmost care and with telling effect. Her tones as always were rich and beautiful. But somehow, set in the midst of this rather uneventful production, her Pamina did not quite glow with all the warmth buried in the role."

When Leontyne Price sang the leading female role in *Don Giovanni* in May 1964 with the Metropolitan Opera Company in Atlanta, Georgia, the performance drew a sellout crowd of 4,600. Before she agreed to perform there she had been assured that both the cast and audience would be integrated.

Noble Arnold, manager of the Fox Theater, said before the performance that about a dozen persons had lined up at the box office during the day "on the chance of grabbing a returned ticket." The theater, which is used by the Metropolitan when it performs in Atlanta was desegregated at the beginning of the 1962 opera season. Negroes had been appearing in casts in Atlanta, but Miss Price was the first to sing in a leading role.

She won enthusiastic applause and after her final curtain call she was besieged by dozens of her admirers backstage. Among the several persons received in her dressing room were Dr. and Mrs. Martin Luther King, Jr. and some of his associates.

"I'm so thrilled," remarked Miss Price. "It brought tears to my eyes."

Dr. King, President of the Southern Leadership Conference, said to the artist: "You will never know what you did for Atlanta. I was so thrilled at the response. This was a genuine expression of appreciation—and about 95 percent of the audience was white."

Miss Price told Dr. King ad his group how much she enjoyed her Atlanta debut. "It is my first visit but I assure you not my last," she said candidly. Referring to Dr. King as "a prince," she stated that she wanted to write to him.

Miss Price told Dr. King and his group how much she give autographs to the fans. In the past she had refused to sing in Atlanta until she could drive from the airport in an unsegregated taxi, eat in an unsegregated restaurant and stay in an unsegregated hotel.

Leontyne Price made her first appearance as Fiordiligi at the Met on January 30, 1965. Appearing in Alfred Lunt's production which dated from the 1951-52 season, the opera was given a fresh touch-up by Mr. Lunt himself.

Richard Tucker recreated the role of Ferrando, Rosalind Elias was cast as Dorabella, with Roberta Peters as Despina and Theodor Uppman as Gugielmo. Unlike Leontyne, all had been cast in their roles before.

Raymond Ericson, in his review in the *New York Times,* duly praised all the principals. "As for Miss Price," he wrote, "she was often glorious in sound, particularly as the voice went up or when she modulated the tone in the ensembles. In her two big technically formidable arias she sang admirably but with some caution. The brilliant drive that she brought to her performances of Donna Anna in *Don Giovanni,* for example, were lacking. The soprano also won some deserved laughs for the deadpan way in which she handled bits of stage business."

"I would like to concentrate on Verdi's heroines, and still go on singing Mozart because Mozart keeps the voice fresh, flexible and focused," Miss Price commented later.

"I am not suggesting that Mozart is simple, merely that the technique is quite different."

They had fun doing *Cosi Fan Tutte*. Leontyne, normally a great tragedian singer, turned to comedy in *Cosi* which is a completely different form of music drama. Fiordiligi can be very funny and is a change in temperament from most of the Verdi heroines.

Leontyne was determined to get the knack of this challenging role. Rosalind Elias remembered everything from the earlier staging. Th two singers went down to Leontyne's house on Vandam Street. Pat Tabernia, the stage director, went along with them. He brought the parasols and all the props down to the house. After having a bite to eat, they worked all night long.

When they went to the theater the next day, they were perfect. Leontyne and Rosalind coordinated perfectly: What Rosalind was doing on the left, Leontyne was doing on the right; what Rosalind was doing on right, Leontyne was doing on the left. Mr. Lunt had no idea that they had been working all night long. He was so impressed with their perfection in timing that he commented with enthusiasm: "Oh, it's so nice to leave it to the integrity of the artists. You see how they can perform and how they can themselves imagine and create as they go along."

CHAPTER VIII

OPERA AT LINCOLN CENTER

It was exactly seven-thirty in the evening of September 16, 1966, when the dazzling Austrian chandeliers started to ascend gradually toward the ceiling. Although the new Metropolitan Opera House was left in semi-darkness, by the time they had reached the top, the enthusiastic audience was aglow. Opera lovers had assembled from all parts of the world to witness the christening of the world's most lavish lyric theatre. From the time the idea for a new house was born back in 1964, the world's most reputable fashion creators had been at work readying their clients for the opening night.

Almost twenty months had passed since Bethlehem Steel raised a beam to its position at the top of the new opera house. About one hundred curious spectators stood by intently observing the topping out ceremony. Leontyne Price and Robert Merrill were present to pull cords attached to brass bells raising the American flag over the building.

The opening of the new house was the most important event in the history of the distinguished organization. "I'm proud and grateful that it has fallen to me to guide the company from the beloved old building on Thirty-ninth Street to its new quarters at Lincoln Center Plaza," said Rudolf Bing, General Manager.

Mr. Bing knew from the beginning that he wanted to open the new theatre with a brand new American opera. He also knew that he wanted Leontyne Price to have the honor of opening the house. Even before the opera was chosen, it was already decided that she was to sing the principal female role. She was the leading American female of the lyric theatre and the one with the most worldwide reputation. Although lots of jealousies would develop among many sopranos, the opera was to be written expressly with Miss Price's voice in mind.

To be given the honor of singing the leading role in an internationally renowned opera house on opening night is one of the greatest prizes to be awarded a prima donna. An even greater honor is to be selected to open a brand new opera house. Few are the singers who have done either, and even fewer are those who have done both. In addition to opening the old Methopolitan's 1961-62 season, Leontyne Price was accorded the special privilege of christening the venerable ensemble in its new location.

From the outset, Samuel Barber was the favored choice to write the music for the new opera. Among his many compositions, opera was conspiciously missing until the Metropolitan commissioned him to write *Vanessa*. This work was presented during the 1957-58 season. Although it won him the Pulitzer Prize in 1958, Barber went into operatic retirement. Rudolf Bing, cognizant of the talent possessed by Barber, made continual overtures for him to compose more music dramas. In an effort to stimulate the composer, Barber was invited to the Met to hear singers, observe conductors and watch performances. It was hoped that a desire for more operatic creativity would eventually unravel. However, exposure was not enough to persuade the composer to take on this responsibility. A very stimulating composer, Samuel Barber is particularly sensitive to the human voice. He writes a beautiful line with real empathy for the vocal instrument. He and Leontyne are very close friends and she knows every work he has written. In fact, she has been exuberant about him since the day he came into her professional life when she was engaged to sing the world's premiere of his "Hermit Songs."

"Mr. Barber writes for each voice with such consideration," Miss Price remarked. "Every note is just right for me.

As an artist, this is two-thirds of the job—not having to adjust your voice to a score."

Rudolf Bing continued unsuccessfully his pleading with Samuel Barber to write an opera for the premiere. Finally, somewhere out in the Atlantic on an ocean liner, the reluctant Mr. Barber conceded. At first he was willing to write an opera to be sung during the opening season, but not for opening night.

After Mr. Barber agreed to cooperate fully with Mr. Bing, the next big problem was the selection of an opera. When Conductor Thomas Schippers was approached, he insisted that it must be a new opera and it must be American.

James Baldwin and Tennessee Williams were approached to write a libretto. Both writers expressed a sincere interest. However, Mr. Baldwin became seriously involved in the civil rights movement and Mr. Williams wanted Mr. Barber to salvage one of his unsuccessful plays.

It was finally agreed that *Antony and Cleopatra*, a three-act opera, would be written for the premiere. Barber, who had remained detached and tried to avoid such an enormous commitment, reconsidered after the pressure continued to mount. He finally called to say that he had decided to accept the commission.

"I only did it because I realize that none of my friends would talk to me any more if I didn't," he said in one of his typical Barberesque understatements.

Franco Zeffirelli, the noted young Italian director-designer, adapted the text of the Shakespearean masterpiece. He also staged and designed the opera. The only non-American in the whole production, he collaborated with Mr. Barber on the libretto. Mr. Barber said later that he did not learn about this until he read it in the newspapers. Although personalities of artists often clash, Barber and Zeffirelli were perfect together as a working team.

Mr. Zeffirelli was already well known at the Metropolitan. His 1964 production of *Falstaff* had been hailed as one of the best ever presented at the Metropolitan. It took Barber more than two years to complete the score. During the summer of 1964, he went to Italy to work out the libretto with Zeffirelli.

Miss Price was stunned when she learned that she had been selected to sing one of the name parts. "If anyone had told me two years ago that I would be opening the new house, I would have been prostrate," she said with excitement. "And when Mr. Bing sat me down in his office and said Sam was writing an opera for me and opening night—well, I just lost weight right there in the chair."

Leontyne Price was joined by Justino Diaz to create the title roles for the premiere. The production, a gift of Francis Goelet, was to be conducted by Thomas Schippers. Rosalind Elias created the role of Chairman and Jess Thomas the part of Caesar. Ezio Flagello was to be cast as Enobarbus.

Cleopatra was not completely new in Miss Price's expanding repertoire. Back in 1956, she sang Cleopatra in an American Opera Society concert performance of Handel's *Julius Caesar* at New York's Carnegie Hall. However, the performance at the Met was going to be different because she would add her acting skills to her vocal talent.

"I've known Sam for years; we have dinner together, a lot. When I learned about 'Cleopatra', I said good-bye to friends and family, cut down everything and started studying singing again.

"Sam played me two and a half pages in the spring of 1965 and it was great. It was me. Then we went to O'Henry's Steak House and stuffed. Since then I have learned every note until it is a part of me. Sam wrote it for my 'Carmen' voice—the dusky quality of the low voice. Every note is right for me. It's a busy role, I'm up and down the pyramid and then I die in my chamber," she continued.

Leontyne limited the number of her appearances at the Metropolitan to six during the season preceding the premiere. In the fall of 1965, she received the first sketches of her aria from Samuel Barber. The rest of the score was sent to her in parts, but not always in a specific order. The entire month of January, 1966, was dedicated to studying the opera.

This was the second American opera of Cleopatra to be given at the Metropolitan. Commencing in the 1919-20 operatic season, Henry Hadley's *Cleopatra's Night* was presented there during two consecutive seasons.

Antony and Cleopatra opened up a completely new world for Leontyne. However, her approach to the Shakespearean masterpiece was the same as her approach to the Italian roles. She had to do far more work to properly prepare herself for the world premiere. She studied with the wonderful actress, Irene Worth, and went through the translation of the Shakespearean language of the play several times with her. In addition, Mr. Zeffirelli brought in Philip Burton to assist Miss Price and other members of the cast with extra translating. Extensive research was also required as a part of her preparation. One of her major sources was *Plutarch's Lives*. She discovered that Cleopatra was the mother of three children: one by Julius Caesar and two by Antony.

Her resonant voice was in excellent condition weeks before the performance. The ambitious soprano spent a great part of the summer living in isolation. Most of her time was spent reading Plutarch, watching television and studying the score. She looked at television so much that she knew every character appearing that season. Aside from studying the libretto, she went through the whole play trying to perfect her pronunciation, diction and Shakespearean meanings.

She felt that it would be an easier task if she were singing in Italian, German or French because most of her audience would not necessarily have to understand what they were hearing. But since her listeners would be principally English-speaking, she wanted to be certain that they understood every word she uttered. She also listened repeatedly to the recording of *Antony and Cleopatra* which was played by Anthony Quale and Pamela Brown.

"My God, what a work." This was the general commentary made by members of the carefully selected cast of *Antony and Cleopatra* at the second rehearsal of the new opera. Two weeks earlier most of them, except for Leontyne Price, did not know the opera. After they had learned it, they were thrilled. They found out that it held together beautifully. The orchestra was impressed with it from the first to the final movement.

A thorough musician, she learned the music as fast as Samuel Barber delivered the pages to her. When she met with her colleagues for the first rehearsal, her homework paid off high dividends.

"That opera is here to stay," said Miss Price. "It will be the finest thing on the boards. I'm going to be a prima donna and say that I think my big aria will be the hit tune of the opera." Entitled "Give Me Some Music," its melody is the main melodic theme of the opera which reoccurs in Cleopatra's duet with Antony and during the death scene. "Barber outdid himself when he wrote this aria. The melody is like a musical perfume throughout the opera. People will be humming it when the opera is over. It is soaring and luscious. And I'm absolutely ecstatic about the death scene."

The second rehearsal was the culmination of three years of planning, creativity, and imagination mingled with frustration. Most of the costumes were gaudy and the sets were so massive that they dwarfed the performers.

It appeared as if Mr. Zeffirelli made every possible attempt to destroy the natural beauty in Leontype Price. Although she is a relatively tall woman, he gave her extremely high heel shoes with very thick soles. He designed costumes which seemed as if they had been pushed down on her. The hats and headgear were hideous. Leontyne was so heavily decked with fabric that she had difficulty maneuvering around the stage.

"She is so dedicated to her work that she never said

anything," said one of her colleagues in near disguest. "If Leontyne is singing beautifully, nothing else matters. If she can sing something and tell the audience and the public through her voice, that's enough. When she's onstage, it's her music that she wants to give the people and she does that."

Mr. Zeffirelli decided at the last minute that Miss Price's dress was too heavy. She was fitted for a new one only two hours before the opera opened.

A giant golden pyramid, made of wood, had been designed to open up and swallow Leontyne Price and carry her offstage. However, on the night of the dress rehearsal, she entered the tremendous pyramid and had to be carried offstage while still inside it. In front of an audience of 3,800 persons, the pyramid stalled with her trapped inside. It went off its carrier wagon and the huge spectacular had to be ground to a halt.

After Miss Price was rescued, she came out moaning with fear saying, "I'll never get out of here with my life, I know it."

Even Zeffirelli, who is always optimistic about his own creations said; "We are very much in trouble."

The opening of the Metropolitan Opera House and the premiere of Barber's new opera were shared with a national listening audience through the facilities of the Texaco-Metropolitan Opera Network. The broadcast provided an excellent opportunity for listeners to become acquainted with the new theatre and to get a taste of the new music.

It was the most glamorous opening night since October 22, 1883, when the Metropolitan was originally christened. In the glittering audience was seated Mrs. Lyndon Baines Johnson, wife of the President. Governor Nelson A. Rockefeller of New York was present. Other guests included Mayor and Mrs. John V. Lindsay of New York City; Marian Anderson and her husband; Mr. and Mrs. Robert Weaver and Mr. and Mrs. Robert F. Kennedy. The host of other celebrities included leaders of business, society and the arts.

Mayor Lindsay and his wife Mary had hosted a reception on the Grand Tier for hundreds of guests.

Milton Cross, veteran announcer for the Saturday afternoon radio opera broadcasts, was the master-of-ceremonies. He summarized the story line of each act of *Antony and Cleopatra*. He gave a vivid description of the sets and the costumes. Edward Downes, the Metropolitan Opera quizmaster for several years was the host during the intermissions. His guests included the First Lady. During the second intermission, he was joined by Rudolf Bing, Francis Robinson, an assistant manager, and Franco Zeffirelli.

Leontyne Price told how much the broadcast meant to her in a statement just before the performance began:

"I'm anything but calm," she stated emotionally. "I'm grateful to God for this privilege, this honor. I'm exhilarated beyond belief and excited completely out of my skin. I'm also excited too, Mr. Bing, because tonight my hometown—Laurel, Mississippi—is now connected with our broadcast and this makes me so proud. I cannot possibly tell you."

Enthusiasm ran high about the brand new American opera. However, to premiere a novel work on such an historic opening night, was a mighty bold step, indeed, to be taken on by the Metropolitan. As it turned out, the monstrous pyramid stalled again on opening night. But this time it was far enough offstage that it didn't ruin the performance.

Although the evening of the premiere turned out to be a disaster for virtually everyone concerned, including Miss Price, she still strongly defends the opera. "It was a beautiful score and I have tremendous respect for Barber as a composer. I don't think his music was properly heard. *Antony and Cleopatra* should definitely be done again—perhaps not with me—because I don't think you can find music more beautiful than some of it.

"The production was so strangely hopeless, however, because of the incredible number of things to be done in such a short time. Since the last thing needed was to lose one's cool, I absolutely refused to panic at the catastrophic things going on around me."

"It was most traumatic," said Miss Price later. "I don't expect to duplicate the feeling I had at that time."

"I really enjoyed working with Leontyne," said Justino Diaz. Recalling one of the mishaps onstage, he said: "The sphinx was supposed to always move around for different scenes. This huge conglomeration of pipes that was hanging for the whole scene was moving in and out depending on what the scene was. At one point the pipes didn't fly out in time for the sphinx to come around and place itself properly. When it came around, the pipes were still there. They made a huge racket and a couple of wires which looked like venetian blinds that were holding the pipes up broke. At that exact moment Leontyne had an entrance and had to sing as she came in. It was the biggest racket I had heard in my life . . . the clanging of those pipes.

"I had an entrance a few seconds later. I watched her come in. She didn't miss her cue. She just went right on. The pipes were just literally hanging over her head. At any moment . . . I said, 'My gosh! She should get out of the way!' But she didn't miss a cue . . . she just went right on. Later she said: "Well, you know I was sort of praying that nothing would happen. But, if I had to go that way, it would have been a good way of going . . . being crushed by those pipes."

Commenting about his being selected to create the role of Antony, Justino said: "It was significant and I felt a special bond with Leontyne. In a sense it was ironical that she being Black and my being Puerto Rican and the two of us were selected to be the leading protagonists in these hallowed halls and in this highly cultural complex for such an important musical occasion. I guess that made both of us feel good or something special."

On Sunday, November 20, 1966, the Bell Telephone Hour presented a television documentary of the frantic weeks of preparation for the opening of the new Metropolitan Opera House and the world premiere of *Antony and Cleopatra.*

The televiewers, in addition to being treated with a view of several portions of the opening night singing, got a good glimpse of the emotion-filled weeks of the behind-the-scene preparations that preceded the opening night.

Leontyne Price, very excited, came offstage the last time exclaiming.

"Wow, what a night. I can't believe it's over."

She caught sight of her Mother and Father in a small back room. She kissed her Mother and said: "Hi, Daddy."

After chastising her Dad for being up so late that night, she instructed him to go home and have a drink of the champagne that was being chilled in the refrigerator.

"But leave some for me," she added emphatically.

Her brother George who had recently been promoted to Lieutenant Colonel was also there. His presence contributed to the makeup of a very warm family atmosphere.

In the spring of 1969 the Metropolitan Opera House announced that Leontyne Price would sing on the night opening its 1969-70 season. Each time she had been scheduled to open a Metropolitan season, the company has been plagued by a musicians' strike threat. In 1961 and 1966, agreements were made between the union and the management of the opera house in time for the opening night curtain call. In 1969, the cloudy picture that beset the preceding weeks of the scheduled September 15 opening remained hazy as the date approached. Miss Price was engaged to open in the title role *Aïda,* one of her preferred parts. *Aïda* was one of six new productions scheduled to be presented during the 1969-70 season. However, the contract settlement was not made early enough for the season to open on time.

An article that appeared in the *New York Times* on July 10, 1969, stated that the Met "announced earlier that it had cancelled contracts of some performers—including stars like Leontyne Price—to avoid having to pay them for rehearsals for performances that might be blocked by a strike." However, the following day a correction in the newspaper indicated that "The Metropolitan said yesterday that Miss Price was not affected by the contract cancellations."

The *New York Times* reported again later that Miss Price along with many other singers had been officially dropped from the Met's roster. The company just couldn't afford to hold them while the theatre remained dark due to the strike.

Miss Price, however, used her time astutely. She found sufficient time to do many things needed around the house. "I've cleaned out all my closets and, moreover, I'm having my house painted inside and out," she said. She added that her closets never had been cleaner.

When she appeared in Washington for a concert in December, she was interviewed by Mary Wiegers of *The Washington Post*. "I was only under stand—by contract until November 1, and so I went out on tour after that," she said referring to the crisis at the Metropolitan. "In the meantime, I organized my music cabinet, took some time to get the house in order, things like that. But you know one never stops working. I just didn't do nothing."

On December 29, 1969, the Metropolitan Opera House opened its doors for its 85th season. Its dazzling chandeliers moved slowly upwards and its gold curtains opened for a production of *Aïda*, one of Verdi's most popular operas. Herman A. Gray, the lawyer representing orchestra, chorus and ballet members, had remarked the preceding August, "Our people could do *Aïda* even if they were waked up in the middle of the night." Although, originally, Leontyne Price had not been scheduled to perform past November 15, she was called in to sing on the opening night of the mini-season.

Although the shortest scheduled season in the Met's history, the sentiment of grand opera was omnipresent. Almost everyone in the orchestra and in the boxes were in formal attire. Photographers, reporters and critics from all over came to join all the great names that had assembled to hear *Aïda*. This opera had opened many previous seasons and the Metropolitan had been doing it for well over eighty consecutive seasons.

The cast of *Aïda* was familiar to its listeners.. In addition to Miss Price there were Richard Tucker as Rhadames, Irene Dalis as Anneris, Robert Merrill as Amonasro and John Macurdy as Ramfis. Maestro Francesco Molinari-Pradelli had slipped on the ice and broken his right arm two days earlier while emerging from church. However, he guided the orchestra and cast through the production with his usual mastery.

"Each of the principals was in good voice," wrote Harold C. Schonberg in *The New York Times* the following morning. "Miss Price used her big voice effectively, and also with a good deal of nuance. Her pianissimos and pianos on phrases like *Numi, pieta* or the end of *patria mia* were in the tradition stemming from Rethberg and Milanov, and were as well handled as any soprano today can manage. Occasionally her tone veered to a near-stridency in full-voice passages, but never at the expense of expression. There was immense vocal authority to Miss Price's *Aïda*."

CHAPTER IX

LEONTYNE IN PRIVATE LIFE

In 1953, the year after their marriage, Bill and Leontyne purchased a three-story house located on Vandam Street, just south of Manhattan's Greenwich Village. It's an old Dutch house designed for historic preservation. A decorator came in and everything was done in avocado green and delphinium blue. It was furnished with loving care; however, the home was not defined in any one particular style. Some of the pieces of furniture were modern and others looked antique.

Because of their innumerable out-of-town singing engagements, both had limited periods to enjoy their home. Leontyne's time was divided by four-and-half months in Europe and approximately four months of United States tours. She did ten weeks of opera performances in Chicago, San Francisco and Los Angeles.

When Bill first moved to New York, he lived in the Hotel America on 47th Street. He later moved across the street and took up permanent residence at the Woodrow Wilson, an apartment hotel. It cost more money, but he had cooking facilities. Lulu Schumaker, the housekeeper at the hotel, took a quick liking to Bill. She always referred to him as a "quality gentleman" and became very impressed with his demeanor. Bill was different from most of the people that came into the hotel and he was granted permission to put in a piano.

After Leontyne and Bill got married they both stayed on at the Woodrow Wilson. Lulu became attached to Leontyne also and the young couple adored her immensely.

When they bought their home Leontyne said to Lulu, "When we get to our house it would be wonderful if you could come and take care of us."

"If you all want me, I'll go," said Lulu anxiously. Lulu moved in with the Warfields and was given living quarters on the third floor. A tremendously fine person, she always remained devoted to both Bill and Leontyne. While they were away they always felt at ease because they had someone in the home they trusted to take care of everything for them.

Bill and Leontyne had a lot in common. Both were thorough musicians and one, therefore, complemented the other. When they entered college, neither had any idea of pursuing a career in vocal music. Like Leontyne, Bill had plans of embarking on a teaching profession in music. They used to argue about whether their children, if they were fortunate in having them, would go to Juilliard or to Bill's alma mater, the Eastman School of Music.

Leontyne was an extremely open, sponge-like person who took things in but gave the impression that she knew all about what was going on. It could have been a first experience for her. During their courtship, Bill took her to a little French restaurant on the West Side of Sixth Avenue in the fifties. Bill suggested frogs' legs and both agreed to order them. It was not until about a year later in their marriage that Leontyne told Bill that she'd never eaten frogs' legs before that time and that she was absolutely frightened that she was going to hate them. But after she tasted them, she found they were delicious and she liked them very much.

Bill was an interesting, intellectual man. He felt that if a singer is working with music that has been founded on literature, she should be completely conversant with that literature. One should know the content over and above music itself so as to truly comprehend what the poet has done and what he has said. If one knows the poetry very well and then turns to the music, one can see what ideas prompted the composer to set that particular poem the way he did.

Very often Bill and Lee would get into discussions and he would illustrate his point by reciting ecstatic French poetry to her in the way that he was impressed by it. He was particularly interested in the Fauré *La Bonne Chanson,* romantic French poetry from Verlaine's *Poems.* Meanwhile, it was a cultural rapport as far as he was concerned and only romantic in the sense that the poems were romantic. But to Leontyne they were all just romantic French poems that he was reciting to her. Bill didn't even know until several years afterwards when Lee remarked about it kiddingly, "One of the things that did it with us was that French poetry."

The young couple was always kept busy learning new music. Most of their spare time was spent at social functions. They did not have time to participate in sports. However, Bill used to take off to the Young Men's Christian Association, especially during the summer months, to take off weight. While he was away Lee would do the shopping.

Bill and Leontyne were a very gregarious couple and whenever their busy careers permitted, they did visiting or received guests in their home. Betty Allen married Edward Lee and they lived on Riverside Drive. Bill, especially, loved Betty's cooking and always loved to visit with her. Several married couples exchanged visits with the Warfields in each other's homes. Betty and Ed Lee, the Robert McFerrins, Rawn and Daisy Spearman were among the couples. Rawn, a baritone, had gone to Paris in *Four Saints in Three Acts,* along with Leontyne and Betty.

Leontyne was known affectionately as Lee by many of her friends and colleagues. Very often a large number of musicians were brought together at house parties. Three of the most popular settings for these festive occasions were the homes of Bill and Leontyne, Rawn and Daisy Spearman and the Lees. It was truly a gala affair when all that superb talent assembled under the same roof. Many singers were always included on the long list of invited guests.

There was always lots of delicious food and a wide variety of drinks. The evenings always started off with dancing to the latest hit records. Invariably, all the guests would end up in the living room where the singers were given an opportunity to display their musical gifts. On several occasions Bill played the piano for Leontyne as she sang selections such as *Vissi d'Arte* from *Tosca*. Bill would also sing during the evening. One night he sang the Brahms "Four Serious Songs." Other artists, too, would take turns to sing. Martha Flowers and Rawn Spearman would contribute to the musical part of the evening with operatic arias.

As far as Leontyne was concerned, Verdi could do no wrong; and as far as Betty was concerned, Wagner could do no wrong. However, one night the two ladies did team up and sang excerpts from *Aïda* in the home of the Spearmans. Rawn and Daisy were especially noted for their open-house Christmas parties. Betty and Leontyne did the second act duet scene between Amneris and Aïda. They were accompanied on the piano by one of the guests.

"When are you going to do that part?" Lee asked Betty humorously about singing the role on stage with her. "I'm tired of singing with these girls that can't do nothing."

There were many persons attending the soirées who were not musicians. They marvelled at the melodious singing of some of the guests. They would sit there absolutely aghast at what they were hearing. "Do you realize what this would cost to hear these people sing individually in concert?", one would ask the other. The vocalists really didn't think anything about it. To them, their performances were a simple matter.

Lee was not a hard liquor drinker. Instead of a martini or a scotch on the rocks, she liked to sip on champagne at cocktail parties. Neither was she a real smoker but sometimes at parties she feels it just sort of chic to have a cigarette in her mouth. Turning to one of the guests, she would ask, "May I have a cigarette, please?" Between puffs she liked to sip a little dubonnet or sherry.

Leontyne didn't like *lieder* very much but she always thought Betty sang it very well. In fact, she wasn't too much interested in concerts and always demonstrated a greater liking for opera. Betty, on the other hand, was a recitalist at heart. She thought most operas were ridiculous; however, she gradually changed her mind about some of them. One day Lee looked at her friend and said in all sincerity, "Betty Lou, you could be a black Lotte Lehmann, and me, I could be another Callas." Betty said she wasn't interested in being a black Lotte Lehmann, she only wanted to "sing *lieder* better than anybody else."

Leontyne loves nice clothes and has a dashing flair for them. One day during one of their desultory conversations, she said to Betty, "If you ever want to buy any furs, just call me 'cause Miss Chisholm knows Mr. 'what's his name' at Bergdorf's. He'll pick your skins personally."

"Leontyne," said Betty, "I can't even afford a muskrat."

"Honey," said Leontyne, "don't you know about where you can pay a little now and keep paying forever? Well, I've discovered."

One night after Bill and Lee had been out with Rawn and Daisy, they went to one of the annual feasts down on the lower East Side in Manhattan. It took place two or three blocks from the Warfields' home. The big celebration had the streets lined with all kinds of foods and games. The two ladies were dressed to the hilt. One of the foursome suggested: "Oh, wouldn't it be fun to stroll through the feast?" Leontyne was all for it. There were counters with Italian sausage and peppers. One of the most exciting parts of going to the feast was to get a coke and one of those delicious Italian sausages. Leontyne and Daisy were both dressed in their lovely mink stoles. Daisy didn't mind too much, but Leontyne thought: "Well, that's just simply awful. If we're going to come here and stand on the street eating Italian sausage we could have gone home and put on slacks."

"Oh, no," said Bill. "I think it's great. We are the carriage trade down here, you know."

Bill's field was concerts and that's what he was mostly interested in. He wasn't too interested in opera. Leontyne was absolutely intrigued with it. They decided quite early that they didn't want to get into a rut of a concert team. They, therefore, purposely did not allow the management to get them too involved. However, they did agree on about a half dozen occasions that they would do joint recitals.

One of their appearances was in Philadelphia singing operatic excerpts with the orchestra. Erich Leinsdorf conducted. On another occasion they appeared in a performance of the *Messiah* with Eugene Ormandy and the Philadelphia Orchestra. Appropriately backed by the Mormon Tabernacle Choir of Salt Lake City, Utah, Martha Lipton, contralto, and Davis Cunningham, tenor, made the list of soloists complete.

Commenting in the *New York Times* on November 5, 1958, Howard Taubman wrote: "The soloists made an effort to keep in the oratorio frame. Mr. Cunningham was the only one who failed to color his tones sufficiently, but even he phrased with style. Miss Price was a little cautious in the coloratura passages of 'Rejoice greatly', but sang 'I know that my Redeemer liveth' movingly. Miss Lipton and Mr. Warfield were searching artists."

They did a concert version of *Porgy and Bess* at Lewisohn Stadium on July 9, 1956, before a crowd of approximately 10,000 listeners. Although there were occasional showers, the enthusiastic audience remained for the entire program. "Miss Price's singing has great dramatic intensity, though marred by unsteadiness and a tendency of shrillness of tone. Mr. Warfield's fine baritone voice, smoothly and evenly produced throughout it range, was delight" wrote a music critic in the *New York Times* on July 10, 1956.

Leontyne is a member of the Washington Square

Church in New York City. She has often sung there at the morning services but she loves the beautiful evening prayer service at St. Thomas Church. However, she still treasures her visits back to the St. Paul Church in Laurel.

She tries to get home to Laurel at least twice a year. "It's the only place where I can be at peace with myself except Rome," she says. "New York was meant for work. It's a place to get things accomplished, and that's the way it should be. At home I can relax, eat too much, sleep too much and it's wonderful for about a week until I get too lazy."

She always attends services there each time she is home and the church is full each time she returns. In October, 1958, there was a program for the paying off of the indebteness of the church. Leontyne sang songs she knew that the congregation would enjoy. Her personal financial contribution to the building of the new edifice equalled to the donation of the whole congregation.

"Leontyne never changes," her mother said. "Everybody at home loves her, and when she comes for a visit, she is still Leontyne. When she goes to church she always favors us with one or two songs, and she'll go up to her old school to visit with the teachers. She's just down to earth, just herself."

Although her parents did not retire as early as she had anticipated, Leontyne made provisions for their retirement in the late fifties. Shortly after that she said, "My father still sneaks in a job now and then and Mother finds a baby she can help deliver; I just pretend I don't know it. Well, after so many years of work they just can't stop."

Leontyne completely renovated and refurnished the home of her parents in Laurel. In addition to putting in every modern convenience, she built a room to accommodate Big Auntie several years before her death. She went to live with the Prices after her retirement with the Chisholms.

At every opportunity she heads straight for Italy. In

Rome she has a high-ceilinged flat located next door to several Spanish nuns. It is a small but cute apartment located near the Piazza Venezia. "I have just a little hole in the wall," says Leontyne when she refers to it. "Rome saves me," she says. She adores living there whenever her schedule permits. Her apartment is four flights up with exactly ninety-three steps. It is situated on the courtyard of a palazzo on Corso Vittorio Emanuele near Tosca's church, and the Teatro Argentina where the world premiere of *The Barber of Seville* took place.

Leontyne is a smart dresser and most of her clothes are designed from head to toe. She likes to shop for dresses in Rome and purchase hats and suits in Vienna. In Rome the soprano can really be herself. She explores the ancient streets in slacks and sandals and dines in Trastevere without being recognized. She loves to go through the ruins of the Forum making personal acquaintance with some of the cats that inhabit it.

Most of Leontyne's colleagues not only enjoy working with her, but just like being in her presence. Although she is usually serious in rehearsals and during performances, she is always good company. It's the human aspect of her personality. In addition to the great stage personality she shares with the world, the artists and her friends get to share her intimate personality which is overpowering. It's every bit equal to her artistic personality.

The things that one remembers about Leontyne are the things that one remembers about a person rather than a singer. She's completely another person when she socializes. She has a wonderful ability to enjoy herself.

When she's in a working atmosphere she's very professional, but when she's in a private situation such as a house party, she gets really very friendly and very warm. At parties she lets her hair down and just becomes a different kind of person. In essence, she becomes the kind of person she really is. She likes to dance. Some times at her house when she has guests they play some wonderful rock 'n' roll music and just have a good time dancing the latest steps. Shirley Verrett and some of her other friends just get up in the middle of the floor and improvise.

"I knew her as an artist first and then I was anxious to meet her as a human being," said Shirley. "I found that the two went together. It was a wonderful cohesion. And for me she's really great in my book."

Shirley loves her dearly as a human being and as an artist. They met each other through a mutual friend back in 1957 long before they ever sang together. Every time they saw each other after that Lee would say, "Oh, Shirley we've got to get together" and Shirley would say, "Oh! Leontyne we've got to get together." But they never did get to really know each other as two human beings until 1965.

Dancing is one of Leontyne's favorite hobbies. She particularly enjoys discotheque dancing. She says that dancers are some of the healthiest people she knows. Although many of them don't have a real interest in opera they think it is nice. She says that if one talks about opera all day it can be a real bore.

The years following her debut at the Met she loved to go dancing at some of the East Side spots to do the twist or the mashed potato. Once while Herbert von Karajan was in New York on a visit, she gave him lessons in the twist at her home. They had a follow-up demonstration at the Bon Soir. "I'm not a teenager, but I get a tremendous message out of present-day dances," she said. She mastered all the new dances such as the Watusi, the Frug, the Jerk and the Swim.

By the time she made her debut at the Metropolitan, her home decor combined French eighteenth century style and modern. Her favorite colors—avocado green and delphinium blue—appeared prominently in the carpeting, silk draperies and the upholstery. Like most prima donnas, she has a deep love for red roses. She likes to personally arrange them in a vase on her concert grand piano in the living room which is located on the second floor.

A ginkgo tree adds splendor to the front walk of her white brick house which measures just twenty-five feet wide and forty feet deep. The house is backed by a tranquil little garden which runs behind the home another sixty feet. The flowers in the garden are tended by Lulu.

Leontyne projects grace and charm along with her innate intelligence. The confidence of her great success gives her an aura of happiness. She has a marvelous humorous streak in her and one can really relax with her and enjoy himself in her company. The backgrounds of the long list of guests who have visited her home is varied. It includes college presidents, directors of art museums, artists, internationally-known musicians, actors, impresarios and writers. Her home is especially frequented by guests during the Metropolitan Opera season.

When Leontyne has dinner guests in her home, menus are planned according to the nationality of her guests. Her principal course might be spit-roasted prime beef when she entertains Americans. It is delicately flavored with garlic and herbs. For Europeans she features the regional dishes of her native Mississippi. It is traditional Southern fried chicken atypically served with chilled Soave, a light and pleasant dry Italian, white wine.

Most of the cooking is done by her housekeeper, but Miss Price has a flair for the culinary art also. Her friends say that she excels as a cook. Three of her prized recipes are crab meat imperial, stuffed eggplant and a shrimp gumbo. The latter is a product of her mother's recipe.

"Lee swears that the lady that lives with her cooks better fried chicken than my mother," said Martina Arroyo. Martina, on the other hand, claims that her mother's chicken is better. The two sopranos have vowed to have a chicken cooking session one night to determine which household enjoys the best fried chicken.

Bill Walker, a native of Texas, loves southern cooking. Leontyne constantly jokes with him about the foods they both enjoy. "You've got to come on down to my house. We'll have some old fried chicken, some grits and some collard greens and so forth," she often tells him.

At times she can be very happy on the facade, but deep down inside she can be very melancholy. One night there was a cocktail party at the apartment of William Wells. Many of the noted artists were present such as Mattiwilda Dobbs, George Shirley, Regina Rysanek and Zinka Milanov. The place was packed with singers. Suddenly something went wrong. Lee, who had been seated among the crowd, suddenly said something that was inaudible to most of the guests. She stormed out of the apartment, slammed the door and didn't return. No one offered any explanation and the party continued as if nothing had happened.

Many people in the music field take on so many postures or superimposed images because of what they consider to be the requirements of their profession or art form. But Leontyne is real. There is nothing phoney or false about her. She's a very, very genuine person and she, in turn, likes genuine people. She doesn't like phonies and immediately clams up when she encounters one. Some persons who have met her for the first time have said, "She seems a little cold." That is possibly because of the way the person related to her in a casual meeting. If she doesn't know someone very well she's always polite and courteous. But when she likes someone as a friend, it's all open and all sunshine. She radiates her warmth and laughter which is what most people enjoy when in her presence.

Most of her friends agree that some of the happiest parties they have attended took place in Lee's home. And yet she seemed to have enjoyed them more than anybody else there. She's the kind of person that can start a party at ten or eleven o'clock in the evening, and if there's anyone still alive and able to kick at six the next morning, she is still there in full gear with them.

Brent Hayes, a college student, was working as an usher at the Metropilitan when Leontyne made her debut. He was not too familiar with the name of Leontyne Price nor

Franco Corelli. All of a sudden when she came on to sing Brent just decided that this was one performance he was not going to miss any part of. "I just started getting more enraptured and more enraptured in her voice as she went on," he added. Hubert Dilworth was standing next to Brent and started discussing Leontyne as a singer. After Brent found out that he was talking to her secretary, Dilworth asked him if he wanted to go backstage to meet her. Brent immediately accepted the invitation.

After Brent met Leontyne, they slowly became friends through the years. He found her to be an absolutely down-to-earth and marvelously gracious person and yet very much alive. Since Brent is married and he and his wife do not like parties, he liked inviting her over for dinner with Hubert. He thought she would prefer this type of atmosphere because she would be getting away from everybody and could relax herself.

Brent later became a buyer of antique furniture at B. Altman's, an exclusive store on New York City's Fifth Avenue. He invited Leontyne to one dinner party down in Stuyvesant Town shortly after his marriage and she agreed to come. Brent put on his smart new smoking jacket that he had bought for the occasion. Leontyne arrived at the door all dressed up in mink. They took one look at each other and both burst out laughing and she said:

"If you take yours off, honey, I'll take mine off."

They immediately decided that it was going to be a relaxed evening. Leontyne walked in and wanted to know where the rest of the people were. Brent told her that no one else was coming. She beamed, took her shoes off and sat down on the sofa. She then threw her feet up on the cocktail table and just relaxed.

One night in March 1967 while Leontyne was singing *Aida* at the Metropolitan, her home was robbed of $75,000 worth of furs, jewelry and opera gowns. When she returned home shortly after midnight, she found Lulu bound and gagged on the floor.

Miss Schumacher was alone in the house when the doorbell rang. When she answered the door and inquired who was it, a man's voice answered saying he had "flowers for Madame Price."

"You leave them by the door, I'll get them," Miss Schumacher answered cautiously.

After waiting five or ten minutes, she opened the door. Two men wearing stocking masks shoved the housekeeper inside the house, beat her and tied her up. They ransacked the house taking five fur coats, a number of opera gowns from Miss Price's second floor bedroom. Jewelry, including necklaces and diamond rings, were also taken.

Many times when Betty Allen goes out into the street all dressed up, people approach her and inquire who she is. Very often, when she tells them she's a singer, they call her "Miss Price." One night after giving a recital at the Shrine Auditorium in Los Angeles, Betty was very mischievous. After the performance, seven or eight men on the committee took her out to dinner and she wanted to see what the new Los Angeles Music Center was like. They walked around there and then went to a fashionable steak restaurant that is frequented by a lot of theatre people. A boy came over to Betty and said,

"Would you sign your autograph, Miss Price?"

"I'm not Leontyne but I'll sign it anyway, honey," Betty said in disgust.

The poor boy who was about six feet two and was very thin, turned beet red.

Someone said, "Don't feel bad, Honey."

"Well, I'm not Leontyne and I don't think she would like it if she were called me either," Betty explained. "Don't you know there are about ninety-nine black singers, but there's only one name."

Betty wasn't mad, but she just felt like "doing him in." She then said to him, "Here, take one of my programs."

"You know the funniest thing . . . somebody will come up to me and say, 'I thought you were Leontyne Price, or

I thought you were Adele Addison or I thought you were Marian Anderson.'" Betty stated later. "I don't think I look like Miss Anderson or Leontyne or Adele. And if you put us all side by side figurewise, God knows we don't look anything like each other. And I think as far as complexion, hairstyle . . . I don't know what people look at. They don't think. They just see there's a Negro singer and she's female, she's got to be so-and-so."

Both Bill and Leontyne took pride in their work and went their separate ways. However, it's a strain on a marriage when both husband and wife are in the music field and are not a team. They just did not come together enough and really be able to live together. That was what eventually defeated the marriage.

They physically separated in 1959; however, they did not become legally separated until December 1967. The legal separation came about mainly because of the tax structure. In the tax bracket in which Leontyne finds herself, she could not take certain deductions as head of the house without a legal separation or a divorce.

Leontyne has had no strong romantic attachments since she and Bill broke up. In the past, her most frequent escorts on social occasions, or on night-clubbing forays have been Roscoe Lee Brown, the actor, or Hubert Dilworth. Her circle of close friends includes persons of many nationalities and different professions. Among these are some of her colleagues such as bass Cesare Siepi, tenor Cesare Valletti, Rosalind Elias and Shirley Verrett, mezzo-sopranos. Colin Fox, the Hathaway Shirt advertisement man, Noel Coward, R.C.A. Victor Engineer Richard Mohr. Lawyers and advertising men and their wives are also included among her friends. She has often gone over to the St. Regis to hear her good friend, Peter Duchin, the pianist.

The paths of the artists do not cross very often. However, Betty Allen calls Leontyne occasionally when she knows she's at home. One time after she had seen one of Leontyne's performances, Betty sent her a note. Betty never importunes her friends because she feels that the more famous some people get, the more of a horrible fear they have that most people only want to use them.

Leontyne answered Betty's note saying, "Why don't you call me? Here's my phone number. You could have come backstage, I could have put your name . . ."

When Betty talked to Leontyne she told her, "I wasn't going through all that crap with the guy backstage. When my name wasn't on the list the last time I was there, he was trying to keep out Leonard Bernstein, Mr. Adler and me. I'm not going through all that jazz. I talked my way in because the guy was over-awed by the fact that there was Bernstein and Kurt Herbert Adler. All of us being kept out. So he relented somewhat."

"You know I would have said to come in," Leontyne responded.

"I knew other people in the cast," said Betty. "But I don't bug people."

Betty had a recital scheduled at Philharmonic Hall on Palm Sunday of 1968.

"I'm coming to your recital," Leontyne told her. "Hubert's got the tickets. We're coming."

Unfortunately, that Sunday turned out to be the Lincoln Center Memorial to Dr. Martin Luther King, Jr. He was assassinated the previous Thursday in Memphis, Tennessee. That was the only thing going on in Lincoln Center that day.

There was a time when the opera singer was so remote from what was going on outside the world of opera. That has changed now. Leontyne has certainly been interested in Dr. King's involvement in the racial strife in the United States. Her plans to attend Betty's concert were interrupted, but she flew down to Atlanta, Georgia, to be present for the funeral services of Dr. King. It was a very personal thing with her.

The preceding February her Dad died at his home in Laurel after a long illness. He had been in poor health for a number of years and had been confined to his bed for several months. Mr. and Mrs. Price had made several trips to New York City and other cities in the United States to hear their daughter sing. The last time Mr. Price attended one of his daughter's performances outside of Mississippi was the opening of the opera season as well as the opening of the new Metropolitan Opera House.

Mr. Price had worked at the lumber company in Laurel until it closed. He was as devoted a father as she was a dutiful daughter. One of the most beautiful letters that Leontyne has ever received came from her brother George. It stated that of all the men he had ever met in his life—including some officers in the Army that he really admired—he still thought the man he would like to be most like is his Dad.

Bill Warfield has always maintained contact with Leontyne in various ways and is generally very good about remembering to send her flowers for special occasions. To greet the year 1969, Leontyne tried to get all the old gang together at her house for New Year's Eve. It was amazing! People who hadn't seen each other for years were there. Bill and many other people from the *Porgy and Bess* cast were present. It, therefore, was sort of like a reunion in a certain sense.

CHAPTER X

WORKING WITH LEONTYNE PRICE

"Leontyne is one of the greatest artists of our day, and a wonderful human being," said Rudolf Bing. "The combination makes her almost unique." Miss Price is one of the most respected artists and beloved human beings in the contemporary music world. Rarely are colleagues, opera and concert managers, conductors, impresarios, executives of recording and television studios, press and publicity agents, stage managers as well as stagehands so completely in accord about a single individual. Somehow, she reflects her immense talent and the great confidence she has in herself on others.

When she is in the cast of an opera, she spreads joy among her colleagues. Many of them seek her company and like to be in her presence for rehearsals or for actual operatic performances. They, too, enjoy her company in private situations away from the opera house. When Leontyne is there, a certain security that everything is going to be all right pervades the atmosphere.

Her art is her whole life. There is substantial agreement among her colleagues that she is a gem to work with. When she is present she inspires everyone to work harder. There are days when some of the artists don't feel like working when they report for rehearsals. After working with Leontyne, many of them usually don't feel tired at all at the end of the day.

Miss Price, too, has profitted by her association with many of the unique music talents of the world. Her artistic scope has widened tremendously by working with some of the greatest conductors, and composers of her era. Also, her skills have been enhanced by her exposure to performances of many of the outstanding vocal artists. She, admittedly, has been inspired by some of them. "Giulietta Simionato who is one of my pet loves. Callas is fabulous, and so are Tebaldi and Farrell. From these girls you can get a wealth of anything you want as a singer," Miss Price declares.

She has a sure knowledge of her vocal and dramatic capabilities. And she is forever cautious about taking on some roles that have been suggested to her. When she turned down von Karajan's invitation to sing *Salome* on stage, this was one of the few occasions where she acted contrary to his wishes.

She also has turned down impossible assignments at the Met. Among them are the title role in *Carmen* and Abigaille in Verdi's *Nabucco*. Miss Price had never encountered *Nabucco* on stage nor had she studied the score. She suggested to Rudolf Bing that she ought to see the work before making her final decision. When Mr. Bing approached her a few days later with reference to the same proposal she asked, "Man, are you crazy?"

She never attempts to learn her roles from recordings of other singers; nor does she listen to another singer's version of an opera that she's studying. She always sticks to the old-fashioned method of learning by starting with the libretto and then working out the music on the piano. Her early training as an accomplished pianist is a vital asset in her learning process.

She works especially hard with operas, arias and songs that are written in foreign languages. Although a lazy dialect, Italian is a linguistically warm and beautiful language. Miss Price has the temperament for it and when she sings in this language, her sounds are usually more pleasing to the ear than some of her German or English phrasing. But even if one doesn't understand the language, Leontyne makes one believe that she really means what she is saying. She just doesn't make sounds for sound effect.

The late André Mertens who was chairman of the board of Columbia Artists and Miss Price's manager said, "I first heard Leontyne in *Porgy and Bess,* and even then felt that she was one of the greatest talents of our time. Since then, I've found her to be one of the most intelligent and well-educated young women I've ever met. And she knows exactly what she wants. However, I can claim that there was one thing I didn't want for her. I didn't want her to sing at the Met, which was her goal, until she was ready. In the meantime, she acquired tremendous experience in the NBC operas, working with Peter Herman Adler, who is a musician who knows immediately how to evaluate an artist."

Leontyne, a dedicated and disciplined singer, has great affection for her work. Unless she is ill she is always present for rehearsals. She knows her path in life and doesn't let any obstacles get in her way.

When she's in a working atmosphere, she doesn't waste any time. One can learn by observing her in silence . . . watching what she does and how she does everything. She's the type of person that one can study from: watching, looking and listening to what she has to say to other people when she's unaware of her spectators.

Many of her colleagues enjoy watching her and talking with her. Some of them would rather be silent and observe her. They like to see what she does and how she does everything.

Leontyne is a very tough person when it comes to work and she doesn't spare herself at all. Fortunately, she's a very strong and healthy singer as opposed to the more delicate types who are forever fussing in almost psychosomatic fashion about a draft or a cold. A rugged soul, she can work and loves to work. She has the disposition and the constitution for it. She doesn't favor herself at all and gives all she's got. She works until she gets the job done to her satisfaction. She's equipped both physically and psychologically. Temperamentally she's secure enough to do whatever is necessary.

An excellent and thorough musician, it is not always necessary for her to do a great deal of singing to get rehearsing done. One can discuss material with her and get almost as much accomplished in conversation discussing things as in the actual process of singing.

When opera lovers hear a finished product, most of them don't realize how much work was done by an individual artist before a recording is released or a production is presented on the stage. Leontyne takes infinite pains in developing a new role. She doesn't force it; but gradually lets it become a part of her. In approaching a new role she says, "I learn the entire score and everyone's part in it, and then it sticks. I'm very methodical, and I regard operas as a unity; I even have personal reasons for the way I use props. The voice is a wonderful thing, but I like realism. I want the audience to feel what I'm doing. There must be real activity going on with what I'm singing. Sometimes I think that I must be a director's plague. However, I believe that movement cannot be staid and studied. It must come from what the character is doing and you must have something going on as a performer as well as a singer."

Leontyne works especially hard on her phrasing when it lies in a certain position in the high register. When she recorded *Un Ballo in Maschera,* one of her colleagues eavesdropped while she was melodiously practicing parts of the score in her rehearsal room. "She kept going over and over it," said Shirley Verrett. "It was flowing and she was making that one wonderful sweep from up—down—no break—just that wonderful color—going all the way through —up high—and then coming down without any kind of gear shifting."

"I want to choose my roles more carefully. I want to do the ones I think are right for me and to be thoroughly aware of the character I am representing—what her thoughts are or are likely to be, why she reacts to her situations," said Leontyne.

"I hope to enlarge the scope of my mind and feelings, to take a more mature view of my work. I don't mean I haven't been mature in the past. I have worked hard, always very hard, because that is my nature and I think I'm a little distrustful when things come too easily," she added.

"I would like to concentrate on Verdi's heroines, and still go on singing Mozart because Mozart keeps the voice fresh, flexible and focused. I am not suggesting that Mozart is simple, merely that the technique is quite different."

In March 1965 she said, "I want to move more slowly and give more thought to all aspects of my career—to languages, acting, and voice."

"Opera is a very tricky thing. It demands a lot. You need a day before a performance to prepare; the day of the performance to crack up, if you have to; and the day after to recuperate," said Miss Price. "How can you sing on either of those days? You blow your brains out and are exhausted which, believe me, I'll never do again. I much prefer to sing on my interest than my capital.

"I like to leave opera houses feeling that I could go back and sing there again. With that in mind, I don't do more than two performances every eight to ten days if I can help it."

She always thinks of herself as part of the performance rather than being the one integral part that makes it great. She does not try to upstage another singer when the production is not staged a certain way. She feels that a musician is giving to the public and should be concerned primarily with the art of what he is doing. Some singers try to upstage another by walking while the other is singing. Others try to stick their colleagues in the ribs to prevent them from hitting a high note.

In love duets, one singer might put his or her arm around the other in such a way that the other will make a mistake. Leontyne has never been reported to have done this. Her aim is to do her best. She told Shirley Verrett, "Shirley, singing is my thing. That's what I know how to do. I get on that stage and I do my thing and I expect other people to do his or her thing."

"It's actually in things like duets and certain ensembles that I get, as the kids say, 'uptight'," she said later. "Maybe this is a type of conceit or ego or something; maybe not quite typical but existing ego. Whenever I have the stage alone, I'm most relaxed. It's a strange thing. I never go on stage thinking about what is supposed to come next. Sometimes in duets or ensembles, I'm a little bit worried. In other words, I try to be fluid. I try not to be 'hung up' about the aria which I know is the sort of thing that people are waiting for. So they are tensed, I think it's better for me not to be tensed."

Outwardly, she exhibits no evidence of temperament, but she's extremely sensitive and temperamental. One never knows what she's going to be like from day to day. One morning she might come in happy and joke with her colleagues all day and the next morning someone might come in and say "hello" to her the wrong way. Most of her colleagues like this challenge because she is never a bore. Even though she can be cranky, she almost always is full of humility, candor and warmth.

She has no phony operatic temperament which is usually a sign of insecurity. Her temperament is manifested in many ways and is usually geared in a specific direction and is never out of anything vicious or malicious. An artist who is really secure is never a problem.

One of the first sensitivities that one finds in Leontyne has to do with her voice. When something starts happening to her throat and her voice doesn't sound just right, almost illogically she becomes frightened. During the rehearsals of *Porgy and Bess*, she, as well as other members of the cast, was being pushed by the directorship. At certain points everybody was being pushed to a frazzle. Leontyne was just getting started and didn't feel well. She had a display of nerves.

Bill also blew up once during one of the rehearsal periods. He said, "O.K., I'm going," He just walked off the stage.

The director, said, "Look, you don't have to do that. If something is bothering you, just come out and say, 'Let's stop.'"

Leontyne is a strikingly attractive woman and is much prettier, both from the distant stage and face to face, than she looks in most of her pictures. Her best features are her almost translucent brown skin, high cheekbones and expressive eyes set in charcoal shadows. She has full lips and a broad nose. Most people's eyes give a little, but when she is conversing with someone, she stares directly in the eyes of the other individual. Her hair has very little body to it and during performances she wears a wig, even in *Aïda*.

However, when she sings Aïda at the Metropolitan, one part of her costume is her own. She wears an old pair of sandals put together with Scotch tape and nails. "They've been with me since my very first Aïda," she said. "They have to be gone over every season. Yes, they've fallen apart on the stage. In Verona, I once did Aïda barefoot. It was nice and warm, and no splinters.

"I've often found myself terribly involved with Aïda. There are many facets in the character that are poignant for me. Many times I've seen myself as that captive Ethiopian princess representing black people in situations like that. It's very difficult for me not to be terribly emotionally involved."

She has a seething temperament and that is why she sings the way she does. Most of her temperament is geared to perfecting a performance. However, if she feels someone is encroaching on something she must defend herself by, her antenna comes out immediately. At that point she will flare up. "Even a meek person has temperament and so do I," she said. "I guess I am slow to anger—but I arrive there often.

I'd say this—tread softly with me on performing day." When she is involved on the stage she's a total professional. She plays the part that is assigned to her and is not concerned with painting a false picture of Miss Price while she is performing.

On the day of a performance she gets up late and has a brunch consisting of a big glass of orange juice, two boiled eggs and *café au lait*. At five o'clock, she usually has a steak, baked potato, salad and coffee. Then Lulu Schumaker prepares her a vacuum of hot broth to take with her to the opera house. She sips some of the broth between some of the scenes.

"Lee is a fabulous colleague. She presents no problem at all. In terms of working with and relating to onstage, we get along very well. I was able to get from her the proper kinds of reactions. Sometimes you work with some people who were sort of a stonewall dramatically. But not so with Leontyne. She radiates, not only music, but drama as well," said George Shirley.

"The energies involved have all been toward producing an excellent performance," Mr. Shirley continued. "There's not been any kind of extraneous temperament which sometimes people will show as a cover-up, so to speak, for any inadequacies that they may feel. Usually when an artist is inadequate in some respect then they will cover up with a show of temper or fits of some sort. But Lee is not that kind of person at all."

"The world shares the great stage personality of Leontyne, but her colleagues and friends get to share her intimate personality which is overpowering. It is just as strong. She's just as gifted in her day to day routine with her colleagues and friends," said William Walker. "She has grace, charm and intelligence. The confidence of her great success gives her an aura of happiness. The world recognizes her as a super artist and she knows it. That gives her great confidence and great personal pride. Any person with those attributes is bound to project some super personality," he added.

"She's a conductor's delight," said Leonard De Paur about Miss Price. "She works very hard and tries to do whatever one wants musically. She's just a great human being. I'm frankly in love with her. I am absolutely unabashed about it. Everbody knows it. She knows it probably. This makes for a certain weakness on my part when it comes to working with her. The conductor is supposed to represent that tower of strength around which the whole enterprise operates: the control echelon; the arrangement of these things. He is supposed to bring a disparate group of musicians and singers together to perform with a person like Miss Price at the center of things. But instead of being that tower of strength, I'm very often being reduced to almost jelly because of the sheer beauty of the things she can do with a song. This is no way for a conductor to function. You've got to be a little removed and objective—controlled at all times. With Lee it's difficult to be all these things. I'll tell you the truth. You find yourself just standing there shivering with enjoyment. I don't mask this, I suppose, as well as I should. I had a feeling that this detracted a little from my effectiveness as a conductor, because it's a thing that I know a conductor should work to avoid."

For a long time Leontyne Price has had a warm interest in Reri Grist as an artist. Miss Grist, in turn, admires Leontyne tremendously as a human being. Reri has fond memories of the first time the two performed together at the San Francisco Opera House.

Reri developed respect for her shortly after she heard Leontyne warming up for the performance in her dressng room. "She had a high range. It was a pleasure to hear her," commented the young coloratura soprano. "Miss Price always arrives early before a performance and takes her time getting dressed for it.

"Leontyne is sweet, gracious, simple, unpretentious. She knows what is what—she's a real person—she does not offend," added Reri.

Miss Grist noted that Leontyne Price radiates this same feeling to many of her fans. Once Miss Price was sitting in a restaurant after a performance in San Francisco; a telephone call came through for her. It was a soldier who was on his way to Vietnam and said he would risk his life for Leontyne Price. He had seen her perform in San Francisco and wanted to thank her for the pleasure it had given him and he wished her well.

She is especially noted among her colleagues for her magnificent sense of humor and her love of mischief. One night Mr. Bing went into her dressing room during an intermission of *Aïda* and told her she was in particularly good voice. She raised her head casually and said to him: "Well, that's what happens when you give me a week off."

Another one of her greatest assets is her humility. She doesn't talk down to persons who may not know as much about opera as she does. In fact, she always admits that she has lots to learn. "Her humility gives her strength," says Florence Page Kimball.

Miss Price consults her teacher when she is preparing a new role or when her voice needs work. Miss Kimball never imagined that a future prima donna was in her midst when Leontyne first reported to her for vocal training back in 1948. "I never dreamed it," Miss Kimball said candidly. "I thought she seemed intelligent and had a pretty voice. But it never occurred to me that she would develop the way she has."

CHAPTER XI

DISCOURSE ON RECORDINGS

"The stage presence of Leontyne Price is as arresting as any seen in the United States or European opera houses, but in the more rarefied craft of acting with the voice alone, she has few, if any equals. This makes her operatic recordings superbly effective," was a comment in *Look* Magazine.

Miss Price's first commercial phonograph recording was released on the market in the early summer of 1955. It was issued as one of Columbia's new series of Modern American Music, and consisted of the "Hermit Songs" by Samuel Barber, with the composer playing the accompaniments. Since that time her record repertoire has grown enormously and is constantly increasing. It includes *lieder* recitals, Christmas carols, spirituals, popular songs, hymns, and folk opera as well as grand opera.

When Miss Price made her first recording with Mr. Barber, the recording industry was not completely new to her. As soloist, her voice had been recorded when she sang with the Oak Park High School Choral Group back in Laurel. Even then she showed vocal promise and although still a teenager, her voice was full, even and secure.

"As far as recordings are concerned, there is a big difference between singing to a machine and singing to people. And while I do act with my voice when recording—and it does give you a chance to preserve things you won't be able to do in years hence—there is a certain palpitation to a live performance, an added dimension or a double trip, you might say," said Miss Price.

After her tumultuous debut and success at the Metropolitan, an album of operatic arias started to sell at the rate of 2,000 a week. A similar effect was noted in the upswing of her album *Il Trovatore*.

Il Trovatore was her first operatic recording. Rosalind Elias sang the role of Azucena, Richard Tucker was Manrico, Leonard Warren was cast as Count di Luna and Giorgio Tozzi was Ferrando. This was Leonard Warren's last recording.

Leontyne threw a tantrum and walked out of the studio during one of the recording sessions. Leonard Warren did not sound too good on one of the takes and his wife infuriated Miss Price. She stated that it was possibly because her husband's voice was so powerful and the microphone had to be tuned down so Miss Price could be heard. Leontyne exploded at her and stormed out of the opera house hysterically. However, she later apologized to Mrs. Warren.

"So much of her art is realized in the music of Verdi and most of all in the *Requiem*, which she sings as nobody else in my lifetime has sung it," said Marcia Devenport.

"It's one of the most beautiful things I have heard her do. It's gorgeous," commented Andrew Frierson about his former classmate at Juilliard.

"Leontyne makes me cry," Rosalind Elias remarked about her colleagues's interpretation in the very touching recording. "The voice is melting and it's beautiful," she added.

Miss Elias, mezzo-soprano, teamed up with Miss Price, Jussi Bjoerling, tenor, and Giorgio Tozzi, bass, to make one of the finest recording Verdi's *Missa da Requiem* has ever had. Ironically, the recording, conducted by Fritz Reiner, was the last one made by Bjoerling who passed away a few weeks later in September 1960.

"The particular glory of the four artists—and the recording—is Miss Price," wrote Raymond Ericson. "Surely no more enchanting sounds are coming from a human throat today than those heard from the soprano in sections of this score. Listen in the Domine Jesu to the voice at it enters quietly on the word *sed,* supported only by strings playing in high registers. In the final *Libera me* she does what few sopranos can. She manages with equal ease and beauty the soft high B flat on the word *requiem* and the triumphant march up to a full-throated, sumptuous high C just before the end of the work."

Miss Price has recorded almost exclusively for RCA Victor. However, her voice has been heard on a few other labels. One of her prized recordings, "A Christmas Offering," was made on London Records with Herbert von Karajan conducting.

Don Giovanni is without peer in the realm of serious lyric drama. It has worked its way into the standard repertoire of most of the world's operatic houses. Wagner, Gounod and Rossini considered it one of the greatest operas ever composed. Simultaneously, two versions of the Mozart masterpiece were released in 1960: one by RCA Victor and the other by Angel Records. The RCA recording included Cesare Siepi as Don Giovanni, Birgit Nilsson as Donna Anna and Leontyne Price as Donna Elvira. Eberhard Waechter sang the title role on the Angel recording. Among his colleagues were Joan Sutherland as Donna Anna and Elisabeth Schwarzkopf as Donna Elvira.

Allen Hughes of the *New York Times* was more critical of Miss Price's interpretation of the role of Donna Elvira than he was of Miss Schwarzkopf. In his comparison of the two characters he said: "Certain of Elvira's lines are sung more beautifully by Leontyne Price than by Miss Schwarzkopf, but the latter is clearly the Elvira to be preferred just now. Miss Price does not yet generate the fury that Miss Schwarzkopf projects, and, sorry to say, Miss Price's *Mi tradi* has considerably less rhythmic poise than one would expect it to have."

There were several rehearsals with Miss Price when the recording of "Swing Low, Sweet Chariot" was made. Leonard de Paur was the conductor and also directed the chorus.

Mr. de Paur and some of the recording staff met at her home a few times to discuss some of the details for the recording. At that time she was having some difficulty with a cold. Although they didn't want to overtax her, some singing was also done. Rehearsals were held to a minimum. In fact, Leontyne is the kind of person who doesn't need a great deal of singing to get rehearsing done. One can discuss the material with her and get almost as much accomplished in conversation as in the actual process of singing.

Miss Price sensed that Mr. de Paur and the others had her best interests at heart. She probably sensed also that they were trying to go a little gently with her because of her recent indisposition. Being the sort of person she is, she didn't feel too kindly disposed to the idea of going easily.

Puccini's opera, *La Rondine*, is rarely performed. However, the aria *"Chi il bel sogno di Doretta,"* sung by Miss Price, has become a favorite among many of her fans and colleagues. The flow of her voice is reminiscent of a violin.

"It's just beautiful sound," said Shirley Verrett.

"We play the whole album," said Martina Arroyo. "But one can hear where we have been picking up the needle and putting it back to hear the aria from *La Rondine*. I have worn out two of those recordings."

The selection is included on an RCA Victor recording of arias by Puccini and Verdi. Also included are the dramatic *"Ritorna vincitor"* and the touching *"O Patria mia"* from *Aïda;* Leonora's two contrasting arias of love, *"Tacea la notte"* and *"D'Amor sull'ali rosee"* from *Ill Trovatore*. On the Puccini side of the disc Miss Price has selected arias of the slave girl, Liu: *"Signore, ascolta"* and *"Tu che di gel sei cinta."* *"Vissi d'arte"* from *Tosca* and *"Un bel di, vedremo"* and *"Tu, tu, piccolo iddio"* from *Madama Butterfly* are also marvelously interpreted by Miss Price.

Porgy and Bess was recorded in the Ballroom of Brooklyn's Saint George Hotel. Known for its extremely good acoustics, Leonard Bernstein was particularly fond of the room. For many years he used it to make recordings by the New York Philharmonic Orchestra.

It was originally planned to record the complete work of *Porgy and Bess*. After cost-counting, RCA Victor did not feel that it was a justifiable investment. It was finally decided to do just the major scenes. Most of the scenes between Bess and Crown were recorded. Crown was sung by McHenry Boatright.

Leontyne got ruffled during one of the recording sessions. She was not pleased with the way the big scene came out between Crown and Bess. She wanted to have it done over. The producer was obviously uptight in terms of time and budget.

Richard Mohr was the producer and Skitch Henderson, a very good Gershwin man, was the conductor. Leontyne was most unhappy with the way that session had ended. However, Mr. Mohr decided that no more time could be spent on it because he had a budget to live with. Miss Price was very angry and was having quite a struggle to maintain her cool. It took a real display of courage on the part of the producer to handle it because she was strictly anxious to have it redone. At that point the artist in Leontyne Price was supreme over anything else. Later on, however, they got back to it and made some corrections.

In the past most opera recordings took place in opera houses. In 1962 RCA Victor christened a new studio on Rome's Via Tiburtina when Leontyne Price sang the leading role in *Madama Butterfly*. With Eric Leinsdorf conducting the RCA Italiana Orchestra and chorus, Leontyne recorded the role of Cio-Cio-San. Radiantly sung, it has become one of the finest operatic recordings available.

During a recording session, many takes are often required for a single aria. Leontyne, who had sung marvelously for most of the sessions, developed a mental block when the time came for her to sing *"Un bel di."* She sang the aria once, stopped, sang another portion of it, stopped, then sang a few more measures of it and stopped again.

Finally, on another day, the studio was cleared of everyone except Miss Price, the conductor and orchestra. The silence of the studio afforded the soprano an atmosphere to attain the perfection she was seeking.

The slimmed Rosalind Elias sang the part of the sobbing Suzuki. As she left the microphone, she wiped the real tears away. Miss Price looked beautiful in a succession of similarly styled, simple sheaths. She remarked that she would wear black on the day that Butterfly died. Her secretary, Hubert Dilworth, was also present for the first opera recorded in the new studio. He was kept busy serving cool water and hot coffee in paper cups.

Because of the rich low register of Miss Price's voice, for many years many of her admirers hoped that some day she would sing the title role in *Carmen*. Although written for the mezzo-soprano voice, Carmen is a challenge to all singers. At a certain point in their careers, most sopranos feel that they can bring something new and vibrant to the role. Leontyne succeeded in her recorded interpretation of the Bizet opera. Her dramatic probing gave a new dimension to the part. The opera was sensuously played by the Vienna Philharmonic Orchestra and conducted by Herbert von Karajan.

Raymond Ericson made the following comments in the *New York Times*: "Miss Price, who has not yet sung this role on the stage, would seem to have a most appropriate voice and temperament for the part. The voice has warmth, an insinuating huskiness, fullness throughout its big range, brightness at the top. And in other roles she has shown the ability to project a quality of stubborn courage and calm acceptance of fate that are at the root of Carmen's character.

"In any case, Miss Price gives notice in her initial recitative that she has thought through the textual and musical implications of the role, and the sardonic humor with which she sings *C'est certain*, just before the Habanera, is striking.

"Although Miss Price can sound earthy enough, she does not bear down on the voice too heavily in the lower register. She uses a sensitive mixture of vocal strength and lightness to preserve the musical line all the time that she is coloring it in the interest of characterization. If the soprano could develop a visual performance to match the richness of this vocal one, she should be a wonderful Carmen."

After her stunning achievement on records, many of her fans predicted that she would sing the role on stage. "Nothing could be farther from the truth," she said emphatically when told of these reports. "There are many things that one can do and enjoy painting the character in recordings which are not necessarily your type on stage. To bridge a gap from recordings to the theatre sometimes is like two different worlds because you have to be seen and heard in the theatre. On records you can paint the whole picture for a listening audience with the sound alone, but you have many more facets in order to portray a role on stage."

Among her own recordings, *Carmen* is one of Miss Price's favorites. "When I have nothing better to do, I play a recording of my own, probably *Carmen*. Frankly, I'm mad about that one—it really entertains me," she said.

Miss Price also recorded Beethoven's Ninth Symphony. It was conducted by Charles Munch. Maureen Forrester was the contralto, David Poleri was the tenor and Giorgio Tozzi sang the bass part. Mr. Poleri sang the role of Cavaradossi with Miss Price when she made her NBC Television opera debut in the role of Floria Tosca.

Leontyne was scheduled to record the role of Elsa in Wagner's *Lohengrin* in the summer of 1965 in Boston. She also was booked to sing the same role at Tanglewood several days earlier with Erich Leinsdorf and the Boston Symphony Orchestra. However, a schedule conflict was given as the reason for the cancellation.

Spokesmen for Miss Price and RCA Victor said her withdrawal was prompted by the Boston Symphony's decision to perform the long Wagner opera over a three-day period instead of one day. Miss Price reportedly did not have that much time on her schedule to devote to the project. She has never sung the role in an opera house.

A recording devoted mainly to the final scene of Richard Strauss's opera *Salome,* including the "Dance of the Seven Veils" has also been done by Miss Price. It also contained a novelty, an excerpt from Strauss's *The Egyptian Helen.* It was mentioned in a review in the *New York Herald Tribune* that in *Salome* "Miss Price provides a quality of soaring exultation in her singing," but in *The Egyptian Helen* she "has to strain a bit for the cruelly high notes."

"I like the Price-Leinsdorf-Boston Symphony recording of *The Egyptian Helen* by Strauss best because it conveys a warm, sensual Helen with no loss of tonal perfection and seriousness," said Mary Campbell, an Associated Press staff member.

Miss Price is forever cautious about taking on some roles that have been suggested to her. After she recorded *Salome* many persons were anxious to hear her sing it on stage. When she turned down Karajan's invitation to sing it back in the fifties at La Scala, that was one of the few occasions that she acted contrary to his wishes. She discussed the idea with Shirley Verrett and told her, "Shirley, I recorded it and that's it. I let it rest there. I have had it. That's it."

Many of Miss Price's fans agree that her recording of American popular songs with André Previn does not do justice to that particular kind of music. She rightfully colored them in accordance with her own taste and judgment. However, rarely does she make her listeners believe in what she is singing as she does on most of her other recordings. Her vocal maturity as an opera singer seemed to have been working against her.

The album was recorded with a forty-four piece string orchestra. Usually for popular recordings, the vocalist is isolated in a booth to avoid sound spillage into the microphone from the instruments in the band. However, a singer's booth wasn't necessary for soprano Price. "Leontyne's got more vocal power than pop singers, so we don't have to worry about the orchestra," said Richard Mohr.

The pieces selected for the album are among Leontyne's favorites. "When I give parties, these are the songs I like to monkey around with at the piano," she said. "But please remember—I'm not setting out to be a blues singer; opera is my first love."

In *The Saturday Review* Irving Kolodin made the following comment about the recording: "For an artist of Miss Price's achievement it is imperative that whatever she does, she does well. Her most envious competitor couldn't have done to her what she has done to herself."

On her two volumes entitled *Leontyne Price, Prima Donna*, she compensated for her shortcomings on the recording of the American Popular Songs. "Every phrase of Miss Price's is polished to the finest grain in a way that can happen often in a recording studio, rarely in real life," wrote Theodore Strongin in his review of the first volume. "But Price being Price—that is to say one of the great sopranos of our day—she flourishes in this kind of hothouse."

Throughout this volume one is aware of the opulence of her tones and the seriousness of her musicianship. The interpretation she gives to nine famous operatic heroines, mostly tragic ones, is a major triumph for her.

When Miss Price entered the studio to record Volume One she had not sung any of the roles in their entirety on stage. Subtitled "Great Soprano Arias from Purcell to Barber," the collection includes "When I Am Laid in Earth" from Purcell's *Dido and Aeneas;* Mozart's *Dove sono* from the *Marriage of Figaro; Addio del Passato* from Verdi's *La Traviata; Sur mes genoux fils du soleil* from Meyerbeer's *L'Africaine; Adieu, notre petite table* from Massenet's *Manon;* Desdemona's recitative and "Willow Song" from Verdi's *Otello; Io son l'umile* from *Cilea's Adriana Lecouvreur; Depuis le Jour* from Charpentier's *Louise;* and

"Do not utter a word" from Barber's *Vanessa*.

Mr. Strongin noted that "it is to Price's abiding credit that each heroine of the nine is presented vocally, as the human being she is and almost never is there a single moment of dazzle for dazzle's sake alone. Dramatic honesty and vocal warmth prevail. Naturally there is extraordinary singing and high technical accomplishment. But only here and there do technical feats outweigh characterization. In this respect, Price shows extraordinary restraint."

Un Ballo in Maschera has never been able to establish itself alongside such Verdi perennials as *Aïda, Il Trovatore* or *Rigoletto,* but it has won practically every sign of musical approbation. An all-star cast joined Leontyne Price for the recording of *Un Ballo in Maschera*. Carlo Bergonzi sang the role of Riccardo; Shirley Verrett was cast as Ulrica, Robert Merrill sang the part of Renato, Reri Grist was the Page and Ezio Flagello sang the role of Samuel. Eric Leinsdorf conducted the RCA Italian Opera Orchestra.

"Everybody is in fine voice, and the album abounds in top-notch vocalism," commented Herbert Kupferberg, critic of the *New York World Tribune*. Just as the recording is long on beautiful singing, so is it short on dramatic impact. The parts are greater than the whole, for however admirable is Bergonzi's first-act *E scherzo, od e follia* or Price's beautiful, soaring appeal which opens Act II, the entire production doesn't build much impact . . . But for the most part this is a smoothly sung *Ballo,* and one that sets forth the musical values of the score most attractively."

In a review in the *Washington Sunday Star* on May 14, 1967, it was noted that "Those who remember the glorious voice of the soprano's early day can now revel in the voice, plus its intelligent use when put through all the dramatic nuances required of a role such as Amelia."

Thomas Schippers was borrowed from Columbia Records to conduct *La Forza del Destino*. The Michigan-born maestro gave it his usual lyric best. It amounted to be an all-American cast because each of the principal roles was sung by a United States singer. Leontyne Price was Leonora; Richard Tucker, Alvaro; Shirley Verrett, Preziosilla; Robert Merrill, Carlo; Giorgio Tozzi, Padre Guardano; and Ezio Flagello, Fra Melitone.

"The flow of action is good, although the recording never generates an impelling 'live performance' feeling," wrote Howard Klein in the *New York Times*. "Individual parts are well handled. Miss Price is quite eloquent in her second act aria at the monastery, and her lush, smoky voice sounds well in all registers."

When the singers were being selected for the recording, Shirley Verrett had not signed a contract to sing exclusively for RCA Victor. Since Leontyne had an exclusivity with the company she was approached by the management and asked what she thought about Shirley singing the part of Preziosilla on the recording. Shirley was flattered when she learned later that Leontyne had calmly asked; "Well, isn't she the best?"

Thomas Schippers was also the conductor when Leontyne Price recorded the role of Donna Elvira in *Ernani*. With the RCA Italiana Orchestra and Chorus the title role was sung by Carlo Bergonzi. Other members of the cast were Mario Sereni who was cast as Don Carlo; Ezio Flagello sang the part of Don Ruy Gomez de Silva and Don Riccardo was interpreted by Fernando Iacopucci.

In the *New York Times* on May 12, 1968, Howard Klein made the following comment: "The prime justification of this release is Leontyne Price's singing, which might be said about any recording she makes. But her Elvira is a true Verdi heroine and her brilliant singing encompasses all the passion, fire, authority and musicality necessary for a memorable performance.

"Elvira dominates, not because she sings so much, but because her first-act arias create vital interest at the crucial point. And how glad we are to have those repeats in this case! The *Ernani, involami* and the succeeding cabaletta are *tours de force* for Price who, notwithstanding a few hard driven high notes, gives an exhibition of singing of a high order. Her trills, for example, are most impressive as are runs and other fioritura. Indeed, one is hard pressed to think of another Verdi soprano who can match Price at this moment."

"I was very pleased that RCA decided to record it because the production at the Metropolitan received not only critical approval but what is even more crucial in opera: box-office approval," said Miss Price. "Fans who would come backstage to say hello—and also letters coming to me and the other artists—asked why there wasn't any recording of it.

"*Ernani* is very early Verdi, and audiences like the idea of having—let's say—three Verdis in a season and being able to pick out and categorize some flavors of the composer which are in one opera but not in another. I asked Richard Mohr who is the musical director at RCA, and also a very good friend, about doing it. He agreed that it was a fun opera, very bouncy and colorful, so finally RCA decided to record it."

Miss Price's personal triumph as Cleopatra is reflected in two arias she recorded from *Antony and Cleopatra*. The soliloquy "Give me some music,' and the somber death scene, "Give me my robe, put on my crown" come from the first and last acts. The recording was released in 1969.

In the *Washington Post* Paul Hume recalled how the opera was badly mauled by the overproduction of Zeffirelli for the premiere at the Metropolitan Opera House three years earlier. "Even that night it was clear that among its strongest moments were the scenes in which the composer could let himself go with the sound of one of his favorite sopranos in mind. And while, in the big new house it sometimes seemed as if he were writing against Price rather than for her, this recording, with the original conductor, but a more relaxed situation, makes clear the beauty of the score's best passages. Price sounds wholly convincing," he opined.

In his brief comment about "Knoxville, Summer of 1915"

which completes Miss Price's interpretation of two Barber works on the same disc, Mr. Hume states, "It is superbly served in this its finest recording."

Miss Price did a second recording of *Il Trovatore* in a decade which was conducted by Maestro Zubin Mehta. It was like a reassembly of the cast of the Metropolitan Opera House revival of that opera in the spring of 1969. However, Grace Bumbry was not included because she had recently been contracted to record the role of Azucena with Angel Records.

In October of 1969 Leontyne Price, along with Steve Lawrence and his wife Edie Gorme, was advertised with a Christmas album. Each person who opened a savings club was permitted to purchase the album for one dollar. Many of Leontyne's fans look upon each of her recordings as a collector's item. Although many of them are opposed to forced savings, they went scurrying off to the First National City Bank in New York City to open up their first Christmas savings account so as to get the recording.

Also included among Miss Price's growing record collection is an album of Mozart operatic and concert arias which was conducted by Peter Herman Adler. One of the most beautiful selections is the aria of Susanna entitled *Deh vieni non tardar* from *The Marriage of Figaro*. In addition to other arias from *The Marriage of Figaro*, Miss Price gives her interpretation of works from *Idomeneo*, *The Magic Flute* and *Il Re Pastore*.

Writing about Leontyne Price, Mr. Adler and herself, Marcia Davenport made the following comments about the recording, "These arias bring together three friends who hold much musical treasure in common and most of all, dedication to Wolfgang Amadeus Mozart. To all of us he has given lifelong inspiration and from all has evoked our best work. It is axiomatic that Mozart is good for the voice. It serves better here to consider the voice that is good for Mozart—specifically, that of Leontyne Price. The sound and the quality are only the outline of what such a singer brings to Mozart. There is deep temperamental affinity; an instinctive aristocracy of style that can only be inborn, not acquired; above all a matter of intuition that is intangible but absolutely requisite."

Recording is usually fun for Miss Price when she sings roles that she wouldn't attempt to do on stage. "It does allow me the opportunity to do things that maybe I'm underneath frustrated because I not only will not, but should not do on stage," she said.

She realizes that singing alone is not enough to satisfy present-day opera buffs. "Maybe before La Callas that was the case, but after her, I think that the visual and the ears are very important. People are very intersted in seeing something they can believe in. So just singing a role is not all of it necessarily most of the time," she chimed.

Miss Price admits that Maria Callas is her favorite operatic heroine. "I own almost everything she has ever recorded," she said. "No one, as far as I am concerned, sees beyond the notes and into the heart of a role quite as she does. My favorite complete opera recording is Callas's first version of *Tosca,* probably the most exciting operatic performance ever made. After having recorded so many operas myself, I know how difficult it is to walk into a cold studio atmosphere with those naked microphones staring at you and try to whip up the immediacy of a live performance—but Callas does it."

Miss Price is usually outspoken about her own recordings also. She speaks candidly about those she feels have been successful as well as those she feels have been failures. In commenting about her favorites she included her "Prima Donna I" and "Prima Donna II." 'Right as Rain" recorded with André Previn was also mentioned "because it's off the beaten track of the things I've done," she said.

One of her recordings she didn't like was *La Forza del Destino.* "I don't think I'm good on it," she said. "I guess I knew that I wasn't in voice at the time but I had this determination not to cancel something. It has been a big fat mistake of mine, thinking that anyone else can cancel but I can't because I've been given a marvelous opportunity and I'd be letting someone down. Anyway, I just don't find anything consistently good in my Leonora, although now it is one of my very best roles."

Some of her other recordings include *Leontyne Price— My Favorite Hymns,* and two albums of spirituals entitled: *Leontyne Price—Swing Low, Sweet Chariot* and *Leontyne Price—I Wish I Knew How It Would Feel to Be Free.*

She is a member of Washington Square Methodist Church of New York City. Having sung there very often, she suggested making a recording with the famous choir of men and boys. This idea resulted into the recording of "———— My Favorite Hymns."

The recording includes "Holy, Holy, Holy," "Lead, Kindly Light," "Blessed Assurance," "Bless This House" and "I Need Thee Every Hour," among several others. "Blessed Assurance" became Leontyne's favorite hymn when she played it on the piano for Choir Number 2, the Junior Choir back at Saint Paul's Methodist Church in Laurel, Mississippi.

The disc ends with "Fairest Lord Jesus." According to Leontyne this hymn is rated as "Hit Number One of Choir Number Two at Saint Paul's."

Her first spiritual album, *Swing Low, Sweet Chariot,* is comprised of fourteen carefully selected arrangements. The orchestra and chorus were skillfully directed by Leonard de Paur. Side One of the record starts with "Ev'ry Time I Feel the Spirit" and Side Two ends with "Ride On, King Jesus."

The album jacket carries the painting of the vocalist used when she appeared on the cover of *Musical America* by the famed portrait artist, Elmer Green.

"I have chosen in this album some of the songs dearest to my heart and to those of my parents and friends back home," Miss Price writes on the album jacket. "I remember hearing and singing some of them as a child either in church, sometimes at school, and very often from my mother, who sang or hummed them as she did her work around the house."

Gail de Faria, a fourteen-year-old student at Manhattanville Junior High School in New York City, was influenced by "Let Us Break Bread Together on Our Knees," a selection on this recording. After listening to the recording, she injected her emotions into dance movements. She had captured the quality of Miss Price's vocal interpretation in her dancing.

Gail was given the assignment by her dancing teacher, Mrs. Margaretta Goines. In the spring of 1969, she displayed her talents with emotion equal to the feeling that Leontyne Price expressed in the spiritual. The students who had convened mainly to become familiarized with the special schools of New York City were inspired tremendously.

"The spiritual is a great American heritage, as truly American as apple pie or Boson baked beans," said Leontyne Price. "Spirituals are a musical exprssion of a great people who are great Americans."

Miss Price's second album of spirituals, *I Wish I Knew How I Would Feel to Be Free,* was recorded with the Rust College Choir. Rust College, located in Holly Springs, Mississippi, is her mother's alma mater.

In 1970, the choir, under the direction of Mrs. Lassaye Van Buren Holmes, head of the college music department, made a tour through the central part of the United States. They travelled from Mississippi to Iowa. The tour was climaxed by the recording session with Leontyne Price in the RCA studio at Nashville, Tennessee.

The recording is not completely dominated by solos of Miss Price. Some of the young singers are afforded an opportunity to display their own vocal talents. The lead singers included Charles Holmes, baritone; Larry Clayton, tenor; Arnetta Westbrooks, soprano; Connally Walton, tenor; and Johnnie Hayne, baritone.

Margaret Bonds, who has made special arrangements

for Miss Price in the past, made three new settings for this album. They are "Singer, Please Don't Let This Harvest Pass," "Standin' In the Need of Prayer" and the spiritual which carries the name of the album. On Leontyne's first album of spirituals, Miss Bonds arranged "'Round About de Mountain" and "He's Got the Whole World in His Hands."

Miss Price sings nine spirituals with the Rust College Choir. Alone, she sings "Sweet Little Jesus Boy" *a cappella*. She had recorded it once before several years ago with London Records on a disc entitled "A Christmas Offering," with Herbert von Karajan conducting the London Symphony Orchestra.

Like her many fans, Miss Price is sometimes touched by her own recordings. "Sometimes I listen to my records and I cry; I'm moved from a point of identifying with what's going on. It's the lyric quality, that's all. It kind of reaches; it gets me. I think I have a very beautiful voice, no kidding, but I can forget that and feel that the person who is singing is really saying something. I like the human quality in my voice and, when I hear it that way—when I feel it down home, to use the vernacular—I know I'm saying something too from deep inside myself."

CHAPTER XII

LEONTYNE IN CONCERT

From the time Leontyne Price sang the role of Tosca with the NBC Television Opera Theatre back in 1955, opera has been almost her total involvement. She has had very little time for recitals or concerts. Most of her energies have been expended in opera. When she was not performing in an opera house in the United States, she was performing in an operatic theatre abroad. Between engagements, she made recordings or preparations for other additions to her growing repertoire.

Recitals and concerts are more demanding than opera. For recitals, in particular, the singer must be a real disciplined technician. There's no scenery and usually there is no one on stage with the artist except the accompanist. With all the attention focused on the artist, his technique must be secure enough to preclude any problem of production or projection. When Leontyne Price has command of the stage alone, this is her finest hour.

Miss Price has appeared in numerous concerts and recitals throughout the United States and in many foreign lands in spite of her busy operatic career. Some of the countries in which she has sung in concert include India, Belgium, Yugoslavia, Canada, Austria, England and Germany. She has made guest appearances with the world's most renowned symphony orchestras.

In February, 1955, she sang Igor Stravinsky's *Three*

Songs from Shakespeare at Carnegie Recital Hall in New York City. The program was presented by two newly merged groups dedicated to the cause of contemporary music: League of Composers—International Society for Contemporary Music, U.S. Section. The Stravinsky material was shared on the program with works by Matyas Seiber, Gordon Binkerd and Heitor Villa-Lobos.

Howard Taubman of the *New York Times* who sensed Miss Price's skillful handling of the *Three Songs from Shakespeare*, made the following comment: "Leontyne Price, who has a big voice, proved that she knew how to keep it scaled down and refined in her singing of the Stravinsky songs. These are difficult to encompass, but she caught their mood aptly."

The Laurel community accepted and applauded the success of Leontyne as concert artist long before she was contracted for the Metropolitan Opera House. With John La Montaine of New York City as her accompanist on the night of March 11, 1955, she gave her first professional concert in Laurel. This historic event will be long remembered by the inhabitants of her native town. The program, sponsored by the Jaycees, was originally scheduled to be presented in the white Laurel High School. However, after some grumblings around town about the appearances of a black woman performing in the white auditorium, the Chisholms rented the Laurel Civic Center.

Mrs. Hattie V. J. McInnis, her first music teacher, joined the 3,000 persons of both races who filled the large auditorium to capacity to hear the concert. Some listeners had come from as far away as Louisiana and Alabama. It was a benefit performance and the proceeds went to The Southeastern Benevolent Hospital Association to build a Negro hospital. Leontyne did not know about the racial problems that were involved in connection with the concert until later years. "We didn't want to clutter up her mind with worries about things like that," Mrs. Elizabeth Chisholm said.

Although the seating arrangements at the concert were segregated, that did not lessen the enthusiastic welcome she received from her friends and admirers. A more invigorating reception is seldom seen in Laurel. With a mile-long parade in her honor, she was given an ovation worthy for any hometown girl destined for international acclaim.

The *Laurel Leader-Call,* her hometown newspaper, made the following comment about her concert: "A marvelous range of voice, with perfect high tones and most appealing quality in the lowest ranges, was given full value in a well-rounded program of music; she sang in French, Italian and German with equal ease."

When Leontyne returned to the platform for the second half of her program, the young soprano expressed her appreciation to the audience for their attention, their enthusiasm, and to the many who were making her visit back home such a happy one. "Never have I been so touched; I am indeed proud to be from Laurel, Mississippi," said the emotion-filled artist. Bright bouquets and lovely baskets of flowers, presented at intermission, adorned the stage for the balance of the concert.

When Leontyne Price appeared in concert at the Metropolitan A.M.E. Church in Washington, D.C., she left her listeners eagerly awaiting a return engagement. The young recitalist was equally comfortable with selections in German, English, Italian and French.

Paul Hume, the noted music editor, wrote in the *Washington Post* on October 11, 1955; "Miss Price is first and most importantly a star in the rare vocal arts. Hers was a program high in musical values and at the same time eminently a singer's recital where the voice had a hundred chances to show its phenomenally easy control in every range, its dramatic potentialities and its lyrical expressiveness."

She is very concerned with organization and has always organized her concert life painstakingly. Early in her career, she began to take along a phonograph with recordings of some of the new roles she would be learning in foreign languages—listening especially to the recitatives. Her tours were usually planned so that she could work each day on her material.

The American Opera Society began its fifth year of existence at Town Hall in the autumn of 1956. It presented for its opening production Handel's *Julius Caesar*. The new concert version of one of Handel's most frequently produced works had no scenery and very little acting.

Cesare Siepi sang the role of Caesar and Louis Sgarro was Ptolemy. Leontyne Price, cast as Cleopatra "was somewhat uneven," was the report in the *New York Times*. "But often she sang affectingly, too, and she achieved some of the same blend of vocal grace with human poignance and expression in the scene that began with the recitative *Che sento, oh Dio*, and then, after a marvelous orchestral introduction, turned into the aria *Se pieta di me non senti*."

"I find that selecting a program for a recital is more challenging than concentrating on a single operatic character. A recital program includes various composers and half a dozen songs may call for half a dozen different interpretations," said Leontyne.

With David Garvey at the piano, on April 5, 1959, Leontyne Price gave a well balanced recital at Constitution Hall in Washington, D. C. "There are really two excellent sopranos called Leontyne Price," wrote Irvin Lowens.

"Leontyne Price No. 1 is gifted with a big dramatic voice, full of excitement. It overwhelms by its sheer strength rather than by its love quality," Mr. Lowens pointed out. "Leontyne Price No. 2 is quite a different artist. Her voice is a marvel of balanced grace—supple, delicate, completely sure," he said.

According to Mr. Lowens, Miss Price No. 1 had the spotlight. He was deeply impressed by *In questa reggia*, aria of Princess Turandot, although disappointed with her interpretation of *Sommi Dei* from George Frederick Handel's *Radamisto*. Mr. Lowens found the second Miss Price at her best with Wolf's *Lebe wohl*, Debussy's *Recueillement*, Barber's *Nuvoletta* and Gershwin's *Summertime*.

In commenting about the Puccini aria, Paul Hume wrote in *The Washington Post and Times Herald*: "To the huge lines of *In questa reggia*, Price brought evidence of her seasons in the great opera houses, pouring out a rounded tone that enveloped the spaces of the hall, never reaching for more than lies within her voice, but summoning up more voice than she needed at any other time during the afternoon."

For the first encore she sang Liu's *Signore, ascolta*. She also added to her program "Summertime," from *Porgy and Bess*, "He's got the whole world in His hand," and Doretta's aria from *La Rondine*. When Miss Price sang "Summertime," old memories were brought back to some of the listeners when they noted the famed Todd Duncan, the original Porgy in the audience.

Leontyne Price made her Town Hall debut in 1954 shortly after she left the *Porgy and Bess* cast. Although it is usually referred to as her New York recital debut, she had very successfully sung Henri Sauguet's *The Magician* a year earlier at a concert of the International Society for Contemporary Music.

The Town Hall debut was an unusual experience since she was already a successful Broadway performer. Most singers make the long struggle to Town Hall years before their names appear on theatre billboards. Because of her established reputation, she drew an audience of almost fifteen hundred persons. Many people wanted to see how she would bridge the gap between Broadway and the world of classical music.

Her program included selections by Gluck, Rossini, Mahler, Manuel Rosenthal and Samuel Barber. David Stimer, the regular accompanist, was replaced by Mr. Barber to play the piano for his own compositions. She again sang the "Hermit Songs" to the accompaniment of Mr. Barber.

Although she had sung at Lewisohn Stadium twice the preceding summer, her interpretation of the concert literature was not as delving as that of a more mature recitalist. The reviews on her were mixed but, however, she did not mar the reputation she had already established. A *New York Times* critic observed that "Her voice is fresh, clear and agile, and she sings lighter music charmingly. But her range of expression is not yet wide enough, nor does it embrace a sufficient variety of styles for her work to make a deep impression. But she has sympathy, poise, good looks, accurate musicianship and a beautiful voice."

Mr. Barber admired her very much as an upcoming artist. Later that year he was responsible for her debut performance with the Boston Symphony in the premiere of his *Prayers of Kierkegaard*. "I wanted her for this and asked Mr. Munch to get her," he said.

"A concert is a completely different medium from opera," said Miss Price. "My concert career has helped me in opera because it taught me relaxation on the stage. Moreover, you have to be a different character in each song."

The American Chamber Orchestra, under the direction of Robert Scholz, played the second concert of its 1956-1957 series at Town Hall on January 22. Leontyne Price and Helen Kwalwasser, violinist, were the soloists.

The New York Times made the fallowing critical analysis of the soprano: "Miss Price was not in good voice last night; her singing was shrill and marred by a pronounced tremolo. Aside from these vocal limitations her singing was marked by earnestness and conscientious musicianship."

Miss Price was also the soloist in Domenico Scarlatti's *Salve Regina* for soprano and strings which was announced as a first performance in New City. She also sang Mozart's *"Ch'io mi scordi di te?"*

In November 1959 with Thomas Schippers conducting the New York Philharmonic Orchestra, Leontyne Price sang Barber's evocative orchestral ballad, "Knoxville: Summer 1915." Paul Henry Lang commented in *the New York Post* about the soprano's performance. "Leontyne Price faithfully interpreted the gentle reminiscing, the prayer, and the occasional passionate outbursts, singing with a clear and pleasing voice which conveyed an understanding affinity for the work," wrote Mr. Lang. "However, her enunciation needs a little polishing. Mr. Barber's setting of English language is masterful; not one syllable should give any trouble to a well-trained singer."

In the *New York Times* Howard Taubman noted that Miss Price "sang with such a grasp of the work's spirit that one was hardly aware of vocalism. When one thought about it, one realized that the control and shading of the voice were delicate and the phrasing admirable," he continued. "But one's interest was drawn to the heart of the work's emotion that is an interpreter's proudest achievement."

In July 1966, the eve of her christening of the new Metropolitan Opera House at Lincoln Center, Leontyne Price gave an unforgettable concert at Lewisohn Stadium. One of the Metropolitan's largest audiences of that season assembled for the momentous event. Competently supported by the Metropolitan Opera Orchestra with Kurt Adler conducting, Miss Price sang skillfully and gloriously.

In his review in the *New York Times,* Allen Hughes mentioned that Miss Price "may possess the most beautiful soprano voice on the musical stage today. And if the gods had issued a direct command, she could scarcely have sung more gloriously than she did.

"From the beginning of *Dove sono,* from Mozart's *Le Nozze di Figaro,* to end of *Zweite brautnacht,* from Strauss' *Die Aegyptische Helena,* luscious tones poured from her throat as though there was no end to them."

In September, 1966, Peter Nero gave a benefit concert in the home of Mr. and Mrs. Benjamin F. Buttenwieser, located on New York City's East Side. About one hundred fifty persons paid fifty dollars per ticket. Proceeds went toward the building of a school of arts in Harlem to house the one which was temporarily quartered in the Saint

James Community Center at St. Nicholas Avenue and 141st Street.

The program was supported by many outstanding personalities including Marion Anderson, Dorothy Maynor, Vladimir Horowitz, Licia Albanese, Zero Mostel, Constance Baker Motley, and Richard Rodgers. Leontyne Price was present along with Mrs. Horowitz, chairman of the benefit committee, and Mrs. Abram Chasins, vice chairman to receive the guests.

When Laurel was graced with a second concert by its native daughter, it was given under the sponsorship of the Saint Paul Methodist Church. An enthusiastic applause from a packed house welcomed Leontyne Price who was sensitively accompanied by David Garvey.

Her program included arias by Handel, Cilea, Schubert, Poulenc and Samuel Barber. A selection of Negro spirituals helped to make up the last section of her program. For encores, the soprano sang "Summertime" from *Porgy and Bess* and "Let Us Break Bread Together," a spiritual arranged by William Lawrence.

Dorothy Cameron wrote her observations of the concert in the *Laurel Leader-Call* on March 19, 1960: "It is evident that this soprano has a lovely natural voice, energy and a keen sensitive musical intelligence. Her high notes were full bodied, resonant and magnificent."

A chartered bus load of music lovers had come from Stillman College in Tuscaloosa, Alabama, for an evening of good music. Many persons were also present from the Gulf Coast, Jackson, Meridian and other neighboring cities.

After a round of resounding applause, Leontyne was presented a check on the stage. She immediately gave it to her minister, the Reverend T. E. Davis, to be used toward the building fund of Miss Price's church.

Leontyne's triumphant Berlin Festival concert of 1960 was not her Berlin debut but a reunion with the public which was still talking about the exhilarating impression she and William Warfield had made when they played *Porgy and Bess* there a few years earlier.

Salzburg's controversial new Festspielhaus was inaugurated in July, 1960, with the hope that it would enhance Austria's reputation as a country devoted to the pursuit of classical music. The "Gloria" from Mozart's Mass in C minor was performed by the Vienna Philharmonic Orchestra and the choir of the Vienna State Opera under the direction of Herbert von Karajan. The three soloists were Leontyne Price; Christa Ludwig, mezzo-soprano, and Waldemar Kmentt, tenor. The latter two were members of the Vienna State Opera.

In October, 1961, Leontyne sang with the Berlin Philharmonic Orchestra at Carnegie Hall, conducted by Herbert von Karajan. Still one of the Metropolitan's newest prima donnas, she walked out on the stage looking every bit the queen of the Nile to sing Cleopatra's aria from the second act of Handel's *Julius Caesar*. Harriet Johnson of the *New York Post* thought the orchestra was "too loud, uninhibited and insensitive in relation to Miss Price's subtly colored phrases and gleaming tones."

Miss Johnson observed a better balance between orchestra and singer when the guest artist sang an aria from Beethoven's *Fidelio*. "While Miss Price's glowing vocalism was more voluptuous than weighty, she did the aria with excellent musicianship and considerable beauty and dramatic power. Ideally, the role of Leonore demands a voice of heavier stamina, a true dramatic soprano," she commented.

In a weekend press conference at the Sheraton-Park Hotel in Washington, D. C., Leontyne lauded Mr. Patrick Hayes as "one of the best gentlemen in the business. The concert manager's courtliness was credited by Miss Price with being the reason for her concert appearance in the nation's capital. When she appeared in concert on May 4, 1962, it was the only one she rescheduled. She had cancelled her appearance there the preceding January due to illness.

At that time she was indisposed due to a virus infection. Mr. Hayes sent her flowers and appeared so solicitous. It was these qualities as personified by him "which I admire in a business that can be so precarious," she added.

One of the highlights of Miss Price's Washington visit was a party given in her honor after the concert by Jean Chisholm Lindsay of Washington, D. C., and her sister, Cynthia Chisholm, of New York City.

Leontyne didn't realize how rotten conditions were racially in Mississippi until after she had left college. After she began to get out into the world she began to realize how bad life was for blacks back in her native state. She went home to give a concert in Laurel for the benefit of her church. However, there were no racial incidents to mar the event. She appeared before an integrated audience on January 27, 1963, who wildly applauded and cheered her. Only two hundred miles away from Laurel at the University of Mississippi, riots had broken out the preceding fall because of the admission of James Howard Meredith to that institution.

Leontyne, appearing in a benefit concert for the Saint Paul Methodist Church, received two standing ovations from the audience that overflowed into the aisles and onto the stage. In order to accommodate other listeners, her voice was piped into another room of the edifice.

About two thousand persons had come from ten states to hear the concert of operatic arias, hymns and spirituals in the Negro school auditorium. Lawyers, doctors, educators and musicians of both the black and white race came from every part of Mississippi to hear her.

Captain James Sellers, who was on duty outside the school with two other officers, could not remember any other integrated event in Laurel except for one previous performance by Miss Price.

The beaming singer remained long after the concert to satisfy her fans by signing autographs. "If I am accepted as an artist," she said, "then I have said a lot for my people."

The concert had been held to pay for a new church and parsonage completed a month earlier. The Reverend Henry C. Clay, the pastor, reported that the performance had raised $4,000.

Leontyne was interviewed in the living room at the home of the Chisholms by Connie Richards of the *Memphis Commercial Appeal*. She discussed her phenomenal career at the Metropolitan in spite of the constant noise in the background. Telephone calls from newsmen in nearby towns continued to flow in. Persistent persons were also among the callers making last-minute efforts to obtain tickets for the concert.

When someone admired the deep green skirt and sweater she was wearing, she smiled politely and said: "Everything I own is green. I've decorated a house in New York and it's full of green. It's partly the influence of the Chisholm home I used to come up and visit, and lots of the things I admired I've carried out in my own home. I'm not flamboyant and I'm not showing off. You do want to show that you've learned things in a few years, though."

"She's just being modest," said Mrs. Chisholm. "Her home is beautiful. She planned it herself and has many lovely things that people have given to her. Leontyne has the kind of natural warm personality that makes people want to do things for her."

At Carnegie Hall in April 1965, Leontyne sang her first New York concert since her Town Hall debut in 1954. The concert was given in memory of André Mertens, her former booking agent and former chairman of the board of Columbia Artists Management. Almost three thousand of her fans turned out filling every seat of the auditorium.

Accompaned by David Garvey, her broad selection of songs from noted composers and arias were by Handel, Hoiby, Brahms, Giordano, Foulenc and Barber. "Like many opera singers, Miss Price operates best at a high vocal level," wrote Harold C. Schonberg in the *New York Times*. "She is used to throwing her big voice in an uninhibited

176

manner, and it came as no great surprise that the *Mamma morte* aria from Giordano's *Andrea Chénier* provided the best vocalism of the evening. There Miss Price sounded comfortable and at home, and her full-throated singing approximated what she can do on the operatic stage.

"Most of the program, however, consisted of songs. It was there the soprano not only had trouble with the style of the music; she even had vocal troubles. Hers is not a voice that easily throttles down. As it was, she did very little pianissimo singing during the recital, but even at mezzo-forte levels, her voice sounded edgy and shrill, without the sheen characteristic of her singing."

Enthusiasm of the evening was intensified when she sang a group of Negro spirituals at the end of her program.

The proceeds of the concert were shared by the Southern Christian Leadership Conference, headed by Dr. Martin Luther King, Jr.; the National Association for the Advancement of Colored People; and the United Nations.

Kurt Adler and the orchestra accompanied her when she appeared in concert at Lewisohn Stadium in late July 1966 and sang arias by Mozart, Verdi and Cilea. Jay S. Harrison of the *New York Post* had observed at her Town Hall debut that "it was obvious that Miss Price was an artist to whom song is as natural as flight is to a bird; but she was, somehow, not able to let loose or to engage herself completely in the cross-pollination that takes place when words are set to music. That condition, of course, has long since been sanded away. What was doubly important at last night's event, however, is that she treated every number as though it were being sung at an opening at the Metropolitan, not in the sultry, noise-ridden circumstances of a Lewisohn hoe-down."

"Let me go out on a limb and declare that Leontyne Price owns what I believe is the most beautiful soprano voice in the world today," wrote Noel Goodwin in London's *Daily Express.*

Before a crowded audience at the Royal Albert Hall,

Miss Price gave her first British concert performance. Except on recordings, Londoners had not been favored with Miss Price since her stunning characterization of Aïda in the late nineteen fifties. John Higgins noted in the *Financial Times* that the prima donna "has a glorious voice, and the intelligence to go with it. Leontyne is a complete singer," Mr. Higgins continued. "The voice has none of those dead patches, none of those switches of gear when moving down to the bottom register; the breathing and phrasing are almost impeccable; the sustained, glimmering high notes recall an earlier and more golden age."

The Sunday night operatic recital was dedicated to the memory of Dr. Martin Luther King Jr., and Robert F. Kennedy, both of whom had recently been fatally wounded by assassins' bullets. Miss Price skillfully prefaced the program with an unaccompanied Negro spiritual—"This Little Light of Mine," while the audience stood. Afterwards, there was a moment's silence before the actual concert began.

She then moved dramatically into ther program of operatic arias. "Whether it was Verdi, Puccini and Cilea or Massenet and Charpentier, to each Miss Price brought a golden-voiced ravishing tone and the purest legato line, matched by her much-praised gift of feeling herself, with the most natural ease, into various styles," commented Mosco Carner in the *London Times*.

She sang at a benefit in Harlem so that some children might afford the same opportunity she had when she was a schoolgirl. More than three hundred persons donned evening gowns and dinner jackets for the occasion in December, 1967. They paid $100 per ticket to spend an "Evening with Leontyne Price" for the benefit of the Harlem School of the Arts. The School was founded and directed by Dorothy Maynor, the noted black soprano. The performance took place at the manificent Rebekah Harkness House of Theatre Arts in New York City.

The soprano's broad selection for the program included Joseph Marx's *Under Gestern Hat Er Mir Rosen Gebracht*

("And Yesterday He Brought Me Roses), Samuel Barber's "Pangur," Lee Hoisby's "In the Wand of the Wind." Cathy Aldridge, critic for the *New York Amsterdam News* made the following observation: "Miss Price has full command of technique, musicology, and herself. She was beauty in motion."

Among the distinguished guests who had gathered for the memorable event were William Warfield, Shirley Verrett, Don Shirley, concert pianist, Mr. and Mrs. Hale Woodruff, and Dr. Jane Wright. Mr. Warfield approached his former wife, kissing her enthusiastically before cameras and reporters who crowded in the backstage room.

A free recital was given by Miss Price to more than five hundred elementary students in New York City the week before Christmas in 1968. At Harlem's Public School 133, the soprano entertained her young listeners with *Io son l'umile ancella*, an aria from Cilea's *Adriana Lecouvreur*.

"Now you know how I make my living," she told her young, attentive audience.

Miss Price was more comfortable close to the piano. She, therefore, sang from the auditorium floor rather than from its stage. Two stanzas of the Christmas carol, "It Came Upon the Midnight Clear" preceded the operatic aria. She ended the brief recital with "Silent Night." At her request many of the youngters joined their "soul sister" at the front of the auditorium. They sang joyfully with the soprano the last stanza of the latter carol.

Miss Price was applauded and cheered before she ended her final high note. She was then accorded an astounding interpretation of "We Wish You a Merry Christmas" by her well behaved young audience. Miss Price, thrilled by the students' response, was reminded of the good ole school days back in Laurel, Mississippi.

Fresh from seven triumphant performances of the Met's new production of *Il Trovatore*, Leontyne Price made her first recital appearance in New York City since 1965. On Sunday evening, April 27, 1969, she sang in Philharmonic

Hall's "Great Performer's" Series. Her opera fans turned out, packing the house, to put their stamp of approval on one of her rare art song recitals.

The prima donna strolled onto the stage, bubbling with glee and exhibiting pure elegance making it unequivocally clear that La Price had everything under control. It didn't take her long to convince her listeners. Accompanied by David Garvey, she started the program with her only operatic aria of the evening, Handel's *Ah! spieto* from *Amadigi*. Thunderous applause of approval rang throughout the audience. "Her voice was thread as delicate as a moon ray," commented Harriet Johnson in the New York *Daily News*.

Miss Price's program included a first performance of Samuel Barber's song cycle, "Despite and Still." Written to a group of poems composed by several writers including "Solitary Hotel" from *Ulysses* by James Joyce, Miss Price sang them with sensitive and sophisticated musicianship.

Writing about the Barber works, Miss Johnson stated: "They were set in the composer's familiar refined, sensitive style, and were very sympathetically set for the voice. Miss Price sang them, as she did almost everything, with an authority which made us forget the means. We lost ourselves in the beauty, and no higher praise can one give."

Seated in the audience was William Warfield who had just sung excerpts from *Boris Godunov* in the same auditorium in the afternoon. Mrs. Kate Baker Price was also present for her daughter's recital. She had travelled to New York just after Easter Sunday to spend some time in Miss Price's home.

Leontyne Price got a hearty welcome when she took the stage at Washnigton, D. C.'s Constitution Hall in February, 1968. Her father had died two days earlier back home in Laurel after a long illness. However, Miss Price kept her date with her many fans in the Metropolitan area.

Splendidly supported by Conductor Howard Mitchell and the National Symphony Orchestra, Miss Price's appearance turned the evening into a victorious homecoming. As the radiant soprano strolled regally onto the stage, her fans and admirers burst into thunderous applause.

"At the very beginning, her ever-remarkable voice sounded a mite out of killer. In *Come scoglio* from Mozart's *Cosi fan tutte*, there were moments of huskiness, specially in lower registers, and the patches of coloratura were not quite so tripping as might be. It was a magnificent rendition nonetheless," wrote Alan M. Kriegsman in the *Washington Post* on February 26, 1968.

"By the time she got to the two French arias, *Sur mes genoux* from *L'Africaine* and *Depuis le jour* from *Louise*, continued Mr. Kriegsman, "the last trace of gruffness had disappeared. Everything thereafter was velvet and diamond."

Miss Price sang excerpts from *Antony and Cleopatra*. For a concert version, Samuel Barber reworked two scenes of his second opera into a "synthesis for soprano and orchestra." Arranged for the occasion and expressly for Miss Price, the synthesis afforded the soprano an opportunity to display her finest vocal skills.

Howard Mitchell had taken the National Symphony Orchestra to Carnegie Hall in New York the preceding December. Half of the program was dedicated to American compositions. Leontyne Price sang John LaMontaine's cycle, "Songs of the Rose of Sharon." Miss Price was the soloist when this cycle was performed earlier in New York with piano at a Composer's Forum concert.

"The soprano was in fine fettle," wrote Howard Taubman. "Her voice, which has range and quality, was produced with freshness. Her phrasing was full of nuance, and her enunciation was exemplary."

CHAPTER XIII

HONORS AND AWARDS

Laurels have become commonplace in the spectacular career of Leontyne Price. Her career has followed a steady progression or pattern since she first started piano lessons with Mrs. Hattie V. J. McInnis back in Laurel, Mississippi. She was given the honor to sing at the Inaugural ceremonies of President Lyndon Baines Johnson in January, 1965, in Washington, D. C. In spite of the chill that permeated the air of the winter's day in the nation's capital, Miss Price delighted the crowd of diplomats, political figures and ordinary citizens with "America the Beautiful."

Twice choking on her words in the tenseness of the moment, her deep voice flooded the whole plaza when she sang against the Marine Corps Band. As she completed her last note, the smiling President Johnson jumped up to congratulate her as she moved away to the crowd's applause.

At the 94th Annual Commencement exercise at Howard University in Washington, D. C., Miss Price was awarded an honorary degree. Doctor James M. Nabrit, Jr., President of the University, made the following statement for the occasion on Friday, June 8, 1962:

"LEONTYNE PRICE — respected and distinguished artist, you stand today at the very pinnacle of successful achievement and at the very peak of your vocal and dramatic powers. Catapulted into sudden fame, you wear your laurels with rare dignity and sincere humility. You are indeed queen among all sopranos and first priestess of your great and demanding art.

"There are no words with which to describe the heavenly quality of your voice. Critics the world over, have hailed its superb qualities. They have called it 'The Voice of the Century'; they have compared it to a stringed instrument because of its warm color and longline; they have called it a 'voice like a banner flying'.

"Brilliant triumphs, enraptured audiences and superlative reviews have been yours wherever you have sung. Yet, you accepted this unsurpassed success with touching humility, refreshing modesty, simplicity of manner, open-faced friendliness and a warm sense of humor.

"The story of your life and your meteoric rise to fame is, without doubt, one of the most remarkable in the history of our day. It represents the living, breathing miracle of creation which bestows great gifts without regard to station, to race, to color, to creed or to place of birth. Born in Laurel, Mississippi, to humble circumstances, your mother and father surrounded you with a home life full of love and discipline of the kind expected of strict God-fearing parents. At three and one-half years of age you started piano lessons and your parents continued them at great sacrifice. You earned the friendship and love of the Chisholms, your other Laurel family, who saw character in your shining eyes, beauty in your youthful voice, determination in your capacity for hard work and believed, that in these, were the promises of greatness.

"You have triumphed in eleven short years in everything you have attempted . . . from the concert stage to recordings, from radio to television, from 'Bess to Tosca,' from the *Carmelites* to *Aïda,* from Convent Garden to Vienna State Opera, from La Scala to the Metropolitan, which is the ultimate.

"You have disciplined yourself by rigid adherence to high standards and long, lonely hours of unrelenting, indefatigable labor. You have wrested impeccable musicianship, artistry, understanding, dramatic power, and above all humility, from the alembic of your genius. You have the capacity of perspective—you have the courage to face deep, bitter disappointment and rise from its ashes.

"Your life has truly followed Goethe's dictum—'that which the fathers have bequathed thee, earn it anew if thou wouldst possess it.'

"LEONTYNE PRICE—there are no limitations to the heights of your genius—the concert stage and the operatic world are at your feet—you are a superb interpreter of music from the great classical composers to the contemporary writers of today. Last year at the Metropolitan, you triumphed in *Aïda, Butterfly, Turandot* and *Don Giovanni.* This year, in spite of serious labor difficulties, you opened the Met's season with a glorious performance of *The Girl of the Golden West;* the first time a Negro had opened the season at the Metropolitan.

"Howard University is proud of you and your great Art, and salutes you. And upon the recommendation of the University Council of Administration, representing all the faculties of the University, and by the unanimous vote of the Board of Trustees of Howard, I do now confer upon you the honorary degree of Doctor of Music."

Still another laurel came her way before she embarked for Europe in mid-June of the same year. An honorary doctorate of human letters was awarded Leontyne Price at Dartmouth College in Hanover, New Hampshire. When Miss Price was presented with her degree, Dr. John Sloan Dickey, President of the College made the following statement:

"Leontyne Price, Metropolitan Opera, for your matchless art has created its own rival—those who would outsing you in praise. In five fiery years of grand opera you have called forth more metaphors, more similes, more F notes of praise than perhaps any prima donna since Helen of Troy."

The Spingarn Medal was instituted in 1914 by Joel E. Spingarn, then Chairman of the National Association for the Advancement of Colored People. It is a gold medal awarded annually for the highest or noblest achievement by an American Negro during the preceding year or years.

While in Europe in June, 1965, Miss Price was informed that she would be a recipient of the coveted Spingarn Medal. "I feel very humble that the NAACP has seen fit to include my name in this distinguished group of Americans," she said.

However, Miss Price did not receive her award until January, 1966. She was named winner at the organization's convention in Denver, Colorado "in recognition of her divinely inspired talent, in tribute to her extraordinary achievement as the outstanding soprano of our era and in appreciation of her priceless contribution as artist, citizen and person to the continuing crusade for justice, equality and understanding among the peoples of the world."

Included among the nominations for the 1969 Montreux International Record Awards was Samuel Barber's "Knoxville, Summer of 1915." Sung by Leontyne Price and conducted by Thomas Schippers, entry was made by Paul Hume, noted music editor of the *Washington Post*. However, the recording was not among the final selections made by the jury in conjunction with the Montreux Music Festival the following September.

The Montreux International Award is completely independent of the record industry. The only requisite to become eligible for it is quality: quality of music, of performance, and of recording. Mr. Hume is a member of the award's preselection committee. He and the other members of the committee submitted the names of ten discs released between April 30, 1968 and May 1, 1969.

"Miss Price's voice is, for me, singularly insinuating as it works its way into the inside of Agee, while the sounds she makes suit Barber's idiom superbly," said Mr. Hume. "My reasoning for naming the Barber is that I think it is his finest work in terms of ultimate purpose and realization, and I find the Price-Schippers recording singularly apposite to the inner essence of the work," he concluded.

In May, 1963 Leontyne Price represented the music

world at the Fortieth Anniversary Celebration of *Time, The Weekly Magazine*. The black tie festivities took place at New York City's aristocratic Waldorf-Astoria Hotel. The soprano stilled the long list of celebrities and Time Incers when she sang *"Chi il bel sogno,* Lauretta's aria from Puccini's *La Rondine.*

Two years earlier she was featured in the March 10, 1961, cover story of the magazine following her triumphant debut at the Metropolitan Opera House. Bernhard M. Auer, Publisher of *Time,* invited her to the Time and Life Building in Rockefeller Center, New York City. Arriving with her entourage, Mr. Auer presented Miss Price with the original oil painting of herself done by Henry Koerner for the magazine's cover.

Sunday, October 20, 1968, was a historic day for Rust College, located in Holly Springs, Mississippi. Many distinguished persons converged on the campus for an Honors Convocation which launched the "Upward Thrust" for a new library and other campus improvements. Leontyne Price was present to receive an honorary Doctor of Humane Letters degree from the Methodist institution, her mother's alma mater. An overflow crowd filled the Doxey Hall auditorium of the small-town campus. Those unable to get inside watched from opened windows and doors.

Miss Price is national co-chairman of the Rust College "Upward Thrust" campaign, a drive to raise $500,000 for school expansion. In March 1967 she sang a benefit recital in the Mississippi Coliseum in Jackson. More than $34,000 was raised for the school. The largest biracial crowd in the state's history attended.

Included on Miss Price's National Advisory Committee are Dr. Anna Arnold, an alumna of Rust, Mrs. Ralph Bunche, Shirley Verrett, Dr. Arna Bontemps, Bennett Cerf, Cab Calloway, James Farmer, Vladimir Horowitz, Robert Merrill, Arthur Schlesinger, William Warfield, Roy Wilkins, Dr. Stephen J. Wright and Whitney Young, Jr.

The following statement was made when Dr. William A.

McMillan, President of the college, conferred the degree on Miss Price:

"A little more than two years ago, operatic history was made with the opening of the new Metropolitan Opera House at Lincoln Center, New York. Every opera singer in America was eager to appear in the world premiere of a new opera which was to be presented that first night, but the coveted role of Cleopatra went to a young lady from Laurel, Mississippi—Leontyne Price.

"From childhood, Miss Price's life has had a fairy tale quality. Her musical talent became apparent at an early age; at five, she persuaded her parents to trade the family Victrola for her first piano lessons. By the time she had finished high school, she had decided she would be a teacher of piano.

"That goal was changed when, while a student at Central State College in Ohio, the superb quality of her voice was recognized and she was encouraged to follow a singing career. A scholarship at the Juilliard School of Music and a family friend made it possible for her to study in New York.

"Unlike most young artists, Miss Price won almost instant recognition. Her Town Hall debut recital was given enthusiastic reviews and a Carnegie Hall concert brought offers of starring roles in famous European opera houses. Vincent Sheean, writing of her singing of Verdi, said, 'She seems to be the singer he never found, the one he was composing for all his life.' In 1961, sang the role of Leonora in *Il Trovatore*, she was given an ovation lasting 42 minutes, the most prolonged tribute of applause ever given an artist by a Metropolitan Opera House audience.

"In spite of the adulation she receives and the excitement of her career, she cherishs her inheritance with its traditions of hard work, disciplined living and deep religious faith. In March, 1967, she sang a benefit concert for Rust College in the Mississippi Coliseum at Jackson; more recently she has accepted the co-chairmanship of Rust's Upward Thrust Campaign."

"No doubt much of this desire to help an aspiring school stems from the fact that her mother attended Rust College. Another factor is involved, however; her feeling that the gift intrusted to her is not hers alone. When she was young, ambitious and far from wealthy, she was given guidance, encouragement and help as she sought the training she needed.

"Now, she feels it is her turn. 'I never doubt God's power in all this,' she says."

After Dr. McMillan placed the doctoral "hood" about the shoulders of Miss Price, a ground-breaking ceremony for the new library followed the convocation. Other award recipients included James Charles Evers, nationally known civil rights leader. Mrs. Katie Price, Leontyne's mother, was cited as a religious leader and humanitarian. Hubert Ditworth, Miss Price's manager, and Dr. Anna Arnold Hedgeman, internationally known as a crusader for social justice, were also given recognition.

"I usually sing what I have to say," she told the crowd. "But today I'll have to try and put it into words."

She said she was helping the school because education leads to strength, and that strength will lead to real freedom and democracy for the American Negro.

"When freedom and democracy are realized in their fullest extent in the state of Mississippi, they will be realized to their fullest extent in the whole world," she added.

"Leontyne does not need Mississippi, but Mississippi needs Leontyne," wrote Mrs. Hazel Brannon Smith in one of her columns. Editor and publisher of the Lexington, Mississippi, *Advertiser* and three other weeklies, Miss Smith is not an integrationist. However, her papers and her editorials fearlessly called for reason on the race issue. She made the above statement when she reported on one of Miss Price's concert's in Laurel. She later won the Putlizer prize in journalism for editorial writing.

Of all the honors Miss Price has received, including numerous Grammy Awards from the National Academy of Record Arts and Sciences, the NAACP's Spingarn Medal, and an appointment to the advisory board of the National Cultural Center, none, perhaps is as personally satisfying as the night she first sang before an integrated audience in Laurel, Mississippi.

It is not as easy to make it to the top as it is to remain there. Although continually showered with accolades, she never ceases to feel deeply about singing beautifully and about doing something for her race. One of her prized letters came from a high school girl in New York's Harlem who informed Miss Price that she had decided to go on with a singing career because the soprano had done so well at the Metropolitan.

In 1967, Miss Price established the "Kate and James Price Award" back home at Oak Park High School in honor of her parents. It is presented to a senior at graduation who plans to enter the music field. The final decision for the award is made by Mrs. Hattie V. J. McInnis, Miss Price's childhood piano teacher.

The first award in the amount of five hundred dollars went to Chessie Ruth Jones. The following year the amount, increased to seven hundred fifty dollars, was awarded to Mitchell L. Lang.

Shortly after the old Metropolitan Opera House closed, RCA Victor released a special album, *Opening Nights at the Metropolitan,* which included taped replays of some of the first nights of opera seasons at the Met. Although an aria from Miss Price's role as Minnie in *La Fanciulla del West* was not recorded for the album, she was given the honor of cutting the first 2x3 inch swatch from the Met's golden damask brocade curtain.

RCA Victor cut up the rest into 45,000 swatches which were inserted into the albums which went on sale. As the soprano cut into the famous curtain she made the following statement: "May peace overtures all over the world raise the Iron and Bamboo Curtains as this historic Metropolitan Opera curtain and others like it in all parts of our world have been raised by the universal language of music and art."

Miss Price was also one of the artists selected to sing at the closing-night gala at the Metropolitan. She sang the beautiful fourth act aria, *D'Amor sull'ali Rosee* from *La Forza del Destino*, one of her favorite operas.

When Fordham University dedicated its new seventeen-and-a-half-million-dollar Leon Lowenstein Center on May 15, 1969, Leontyne Price was on hand to be awarded an honorary degree of Doctor of Humane Letters. Sharing the kudos with Miss Price was His Eminence, Terence Cardinal Cooke, who received an honorary Doctor of Laws Degree. Miss Price, cited by Fordham as a "leading performing artist," was presented her degree by the Reverend Michael P. Walsh, S.J., President of the University.

"This occasion is Miss Price's second opening at Lincoln Center," commented Dr. Walsh as he conferred the degree on Miss Price. "No tribute Fordham offers her can equal the professional accolade she received in being asked to open a new opera house three years ago. Alongside a talent like hers, and the towering beauty of her art, any mere collection of scholars must blush and remind itself that 'sheer plod makes plow lown sillion shine.' There has been blessedly little plod to Miss Price's career, for all that no art as great as hers is possible without a discipline few mortals could stand and a dedication of which few are capable. In this complex city which can be as blind to cruelty as it is sensitive to beauty, we honor in Leontyne Price a great artist who reminds all of us that in the world of the spirit there are no boundaries and should be no barriers. How much all American Universities need their reminder we at Fordham are well aware. Today, however, at our house warming, we simply want to rejoice in a girl from the South who, for all that she is undisputed queen of the neighboring palace, is still a lass unparalleled."

When Leontyne Price opened the Metropolitan's 1969-70 mini season, it was the third time the Met's principal lyric soprano had been given the honor of singing on an opening night. Very few sopranos have ever opened the Metropolitan more than twice. The most recent one was Zinka Milanov, the Yougoslav soprano, who sang Amelia in *Un Ballo in Maschera* her first opening night at the beginning of the 1940-41 season. She sang the title role in *Aïda* when she opened the 1951-52 season. For the opening of the 1952-53 season she sang the role of Leonora in *La Forza del Destino*.

In general, opening night is the most memorable night of the opera season. All the attention is focused on the soprano. That night, the soprano who sings the leading role is the one who is referred to as "opening the Met season."

APPENDIX A

OTHER BLACK SINGERS AT THE METROPOLITAN OPERA HOUSE

Although there are many great opera companies in the world, when a singer makes his debut at the Metropolitan, the consensus of opinion is that he has really made it in the field of opera. Most people look upon the Met as the zenith of the opera singer's career.

Since Marian Anderson made her historic debut at the Metropolitan Opera house in 1955, her trail has been followed by only ten black singers appearing in solo roles. Leontyne Price is the first of the group to gain a lasting success at the theatre. The black soprano feels extremely proud that the doors have been opened to singers irrespective of their color. However, she has expressed deep concern about an obvious absence of black male singers. "There must be many dramatic black tenors and baritones," said the concerned Miss Price.

Miss Price was the fifth black person to sing at the Met in a major role. She has been instrumental in ushering in a new era at the opera house. Although other black singers preceded her, she has become the first to attain prima donna stature and to remain as a permanent fixture on the Met's illustrious roster.

It's almost impossible to discuss any of the careers of the distinguished group of black singers without bringing Miss Price into it. She has been an influential force because of the type of person she is. She is very much loved by not only the black singers but all of the singers and stagehands because she has always been very gracious.

She has done a lot for the revitalization of grand opera. The fact that she is a leading singer and is a black woman has interested many blacks in finding out what opera is all about. She's an artist who functions in the normal circle of opera. She hasn't gone out to find pockets where people aren't familiar with opera to inform them of what opera is all about. However, because she is a black woman and has achieved such a phenomenal success, she has created an interest in opera amongst blacks in America that didn't exist on that wide a scale before.

Prior to the nineteen sixties classical music for Negro vocalists was limited almost exclusively to the concert stage. The black community usually enjoyed the talents of members of their race in a neighborhood church or concert hall. Negro singers were discouraged from participating in grand opera on a large scale due to discriminatory practices.

When Rudolf Bing arrived as General Manager of the Metropolitan Opera Company in 1950, discipline at the venerable house was lax. He turned the Met into the best-run opera house in the world. Also, during his administration, the doors have been opened for black artists to perform in roles that were previously reserved for whites only. In addition to inaugurating a fair hiring practice, Mr. Bing refuses to permit his company to perform before segregated audiences.

The impresario has scoured the operatic field in search of some of the best talent obtainable, irrespective of race or national origin. "I wouldn't hire anyone because he is a Negro, and I wouldn't refuse to hire anyone because he is a Negro either," said Mr. Bing in defense of his policy. Under his direction a large number of top-notch talent has been added to the Met roster. Included among the new voices that have been brought in during the Bing administration are Renata Tebaldi, George Shirley, Maria Callas, Shirley Verrett, Justino Diaz, Birgit Nilsson, Grace Bumbry, Martina Arroyo, Joan Sutherland and Franco Corelli.

Credit S. Hurok, New York, N. Y.

Marion Anderson

Audrey Michaels

Reri Grist as Adele in Die Fledermaus

Credit BENDER, N. Y.

George Shirley

Mattiwilda Dobbs

Columbia Artists Management, Inc., N. Y., N. Y.

Macrice Feldman, PRSA Acc.

Gloria Davy

Felicia Weathers

Credit the Associated Publishers, Washington, D.C.

Lillian Evanti

Credit Louis Melancon, Metropolitan Opera House, N. Y., N. Y.

Grace Bumbry as Carmen

Martina Arroyo
Credit Thea Dispeker, New York, N. Y.

Constance Hope Associates, New York, N. Y.

Shirley Verrett

In the past, Negro singers who wanted to participate in grand opera had to test their luck in Europe. The first to make the trek to the Continent in search of an operatic fortune was Lillian Evans Tibbs of Washington, D. C. The eager young singer had no sponsor in the Old World and left her native land well aware of the difficulties she might encounter on the other side of the Atlantic. She, nevertheless, was determined to become a success. In the United States the Negro was accepted only as a buffoon in big-time music, and Lillian wanted to exercise the full potential of her voice.

A lyric coloratura soprano, she was in Europe six months before making her operatic debut. Her first appearance was in Delibes' *Lakmé* with the Nice Opera Company in 1925. She was the first Negro to appear with an organized European opera company.

Known professionally as Madame Evanti, she made appearances throughout Europe. When her contract with the Nice Opera Company ended, she contracted for herself and began a career that sent her to several European cities. Her other major roles were in *Le Coq d'Or, Romeo and Juliet* and *Lucia di Lammermoor*. Even in Europe color seems to have been a barrier for the Negro. Madame Evanti, in spite of her success, did not perform in the major European opera houses. However, she was cast in *The Barber of Seville* in Genoa. She sang in Germany in concert only because the government would not permit foreigners to sing in the national opera houses after 1933.

Lillian was heard in Italy by Giulio Gatti-Casazza, then General Manager of the Metropolitan Opera Company. Impressed with her performance, he urged her to return to the United States in 1932 and audition for the Met; however, racial segregation did not permit the audition. When she gave her first concert in Washington late in 1933 at the Belasco Theatre, she drew wide critical acclaim.

Madame Evanti was a principal aide to the founder of the Negro National Opera Company in 1942 in Philadelphia.

In 1943 the company presented an English version of *La Traviata* at the Watergate in the nation's capital. The soprano sang the role of Violetta.

A year later she was presented with an alumni award by Howard University in Washington, D. C., her alma mater. The citation read in part: "When you sang the role of Violetta the audience of 12,000 persons was thrilled by your singing and the city's most distinguished critics were persuaded to acclaim you as a singer and actress of consummate artistry."

Caterina Jarboro, another Negro opera singer, left a lasting impression on the operatic world when she made her debut before a New York City audience in July of 1933. She was applauded enthusiastically by a crowd that overflowed into the aisles when she sang the title role in *Aïda* with Alfredo Salmaggi's Chicago Opera Company in Manhattan's Hippodrome Theatre. Her people came down to hear her from Harlem in large numbers making up a third of the audience.

The young soprano, a native of Wilmington, North Carolina, was baptized as Catherine Yarborough. Caterina was the first Negro to sing with an American opera company. Like Madame Evanti, she had gone to Europe in the mid-twenties. Success came immediately after she sang the title role in *Aïda* at the Puccini Opera House in Milan. The Paris Opera offered her a contract for six performances, and Miss Jarboro became popular in the *Queen of Sheba* and *L'Africaine*. For three years thereafter, she was cast regularly in leading opera houses in France, Italy and Switzerland.

After her New York success she returned to Europe and was immediately engaged at the Opera La Monnaie in Brussels. For four seasons she sang with great success there. She sang *Aïda, the Queen of Sheba* by Golmark as well as Gounod's *Queen of Sheba*. She also triumphed in *L'Africaine* and her fame spread to all the musical centers of the world. Her operatic career ended abruptly when she had to cancel an engagement scheduled for Vienna and return to the United States because of World War II.

Marian Anderson made her debut at the Metropolitan as Ulrica in Verdi's *Masked Ball,* under the direction of Dimitri Mitroupoulos. During her prime she was the world's greatest contralto. However, when she was invited to sing at the world's leading operatic theatre, she was in the autumn of her career. Her golden voice showed vivid signs of losing its lustre. Although she had never before been cast on an operatic stage, she had sung in most of the great concert halls of the world. Opera had only been a dream; for the way had not been open for black singers to perform in the world of dramatic music.

This was the first time since the Met opened its doors in 1883 that a Negro had appeared on its stage as a regular member of the company in a principal singing role. Up to that point, the Metropolitan was the only opera house in the United States that practiced racial discrimination. However, in 1951 Mr. Bing brought in Janet Collins as a prima ballerina. She became the first Negro to perform in a major role at the Metropolitan.

Miss Anderson had already enjoyed a long and triumphant career. In 1938 she gave seventy recitals in the United States—the longest, most intensive tour in concert history for any singer. On June 10 of that year, Howard University in Washington, D. C., conferred upon her an Honorary Doctorate of Music. That same month she also received the Spingarn Medal of the National Association for the Advancement of Colored People.

In 1939 she became a national issue when Constitution Hall was denied her by the Daughters of the American Revolution causing Mrs. Franklin D. Roosevelt to resign from that organization. It prompted the United States Government to offer her the use of the Lincoln Memorial for an outdoor concert in Washington, D. C.

In August, 1958, President Dwight D. Eisenhower appointed Miss Anderson as U. S. Delegate to the United

Nations. In the fall of 1960, she was invited to sing at the Inauguration of President John F. Kennedy.

Another important event was Miss Anderson's concert in March, 1962 in Washington, D. C. She sang in the new State Department Auditorium at the invitation of President Kennedy's Cabinet. The Attorney General, Robert F. Kennedy, introduced her to the distinguished audience which included the Congress, the Supreme Court and Diplomatic Corps.

In March, 1942, the contralto established the Marian Anderson Award. She is sponsoring young talented men and women in the pursuits of their musical and educational goals. Three of the prize recipients, Grace Bumbry, Mattiwilda Dobbs and and Shirley Verrett, have gained worldwide prominence and have followed the trail blazer to the Metropolitan Opera House.

Robert McFerrin got a start when he won first prize in a Metropolitan Opera Audition of the Air in 1954. The Metropolitan guarantees no contracts to winners of its auditions; however, McFerrin did become the first black person to enter the Metropolitan Opera's training school. Entering on June 8, 1953, he worked hard and his ambition was to eventually get a Met contract.

John Gutman, artistic assistant to Rudolf Bing and a judge of the auditions, said, "If we did not think there was a chance Mr. Ferrin would appear with the Metropolitan we would not have chosen him. If we did not feel completely that color of skin made no difference, we would not be so cruel as to choose a Negro to enter the course." The classes, called the Kathryn Turney Long Courses, were reserved almost exclusively for junior members of the Metropolitan company, some of whom attended two or more sessions.

Born in Marianna, Arkansas, Robert was one of eight children in the family of Reverend and Mrs. Melvin McFerrin. A Baptist minister, Reverend McFerrin retired in 1943. Robert took music classes in the public schools in

Saint Louis and later enrolled in Fisk University in Nashville, Tennessee, for the 1940-41 school year. He then became a student at the Chicago Musical College during the 1941-42 school year. His vocal training was interrupted at the College while he served in the Army of the United States from 1942 to 1946. However, he returned to the Chicago institution where he studied during the period of 1946 to 1948.

He subsequently appeared in Chicago's summer Grant Park series and won a scholarship in the Opera Department at Tanglewood in the summer of 1949. In 1950, he sang the leading role of Orestes in *Iphigenia in Tauris* with the New England Opera Company in Boston. The young baritone later sang Valentin in *Faust* and the title role in *Rigoletto* with the same company. He sang in recitals throughout the United States and also made his debut in New York's Town Hall in 1950.

On January 27, 1955, Robert McFerrin made his debut at the Metropolitan. He performed in a production of *Aïda*. Although Marian Anderson had been heard twenty days before him, her part was not a starring role. With his debut as Amonasro, the Ethiopian King, Robert McFerrin became the first black male singer to be cast in a leading role at the Metropolitan.

"If there had been others before me, my whole approach to a career would have been differnt," Mr. McFerrin said. "All of those years I was concentrating on concert work I could have been learning operatic roles. But the thought never occurred to me that there might be a chance. The opportunity just didn't exist for Negroes."

On February 15, 1955, the following statement appeared in *Musical America* about Mr. McFerrin's debut performance: "The repetition of Verdi's opera has as its principal feature the debut with the company of Robert McFerrin as Amonasro. This capable young baritone is the second Negro artist to be heard with the company . . . Mr. McFerrin has a smooth rich voice with a virile timbre, if only a bit light for this role. Winner of 1953 Auditions of the Air, he sang with refined artistry, making a particular impression with his resonant top tones, though he needed greater dramatic forcefulness."

Gloria Davy made her debut at the Metropolitan in the title role of *Aïda* in 1958. That same season, she also sang the roles of Leonora in *Il Trovatore,* Pamina in the *Magic Flute* and Nedda in *Pagliacci.*

Her brilliant interpretation of *Aïda* quickly spread throughout the music world. She had first sung it in Nice, France. Herbert von Karajan invited her to sing the role with him at the Vienna State Opera in Convent Garden. "Vocally as physically, she is a striking Aïda," observed *The London Times.* Miss Davy also sang with Wieland Wagner at the Deutsche Oper Berlin and became a permanent member of the company in 1963.

Her repertoire includes concert music and operatic compositions ranging from Purcell, Handel, Gluck and Mozart to Rossini, Donizetti, Verdi, Puccini and Strauss. She also has mastered *lieder* singing as well as modern literature. The influential *Die Welt* of Berlin and Hamburg wrote: "Her velvety, beautiful soprano voice, with its lovely timbre, is a highly trained instrument of innate intelligence. When combined with the personal charm of this artist, it presents a rare harmony."

Another black singer who sang at the Metropolitan Opera was Mattiwilda Dobbs. The lyric coloratura soprano made her debut in 1958 as Gilda in *Rigoletto.*

Born in Atlanta, Georgia, she was the fifth of six greatly gifted daughters of a railway mail clerk. At the age of six, she made an unexpected solo debut. She had been scheduled to sing a duet with her sister June at a church function. Eating too much ice cream beforehand, June became ill and was unable to perform. Mattiwilda bravely sang the duet as a solo with her older sister Josephine accompanying her at the piano.

Like Leontyne Price, Mattiwilda spent her entire girlhood studying the piano. She was seventeen and an accomplished pianist before she turned to voice training. It was her mother who recognized her vocal talent and advised her to join the choir of the First Congregational Church. However, her first vocal lessons did not begin until she enrolled in Atlanta's Spelman College. At Spelman she studied vocal technique and repertoire with Naomi Maise and Willis James.

During Miss Dobbs' last year in college, a local singer heard her in a college concert. The lady telephoned Mattiwilda's father and arranged to talk with him in his home about a career for his daughter. The singer's high opinion of Mattiwilda convinced Mr. Dobbs to take his daughter for an audition with Madame Lotte Leonard, a noted voice teacher in New York. The teacher, impressed with Mattiwilda, immediately accepted her as a pupil.

Miss Dobbs entered Teacher's College at Columbia University to major in Spanish. She studied music and earned a Master of Arts degree concurrently. That same year, she won the Marian Anderson Scholarship in voice.

A scholarship at Mannes School in New York enabled her to study in its opera workshop. After a summer of study at Tanglewood and a John Hay Whitney Fellowship, Mattiwilda was placed on the route to Paris. For two years she studied at the French School of Music with the extraordinary Pierre Bernac.

Mattiwilda Dobbs became the first black singer ever to sing at La Scala in Milan when she made her memorable debut as Elvira in Rossini's *L'Italiana in Algeri*. That same year she was engaged at Covent Garden after her great success as Zerbinetta in *Ariadne auf Naxos*. The role of Zerbinetta brought her to New York for her triumphant debut with the Little Orchestra Society.

The singer shares her time between her native country and the Continent. She has established a home in Hamburg where she is the leading coloratura soprano of the State Opera in Hamburg. Her repertoire is extensive and varied.

It includes the roles of Olympia in the *Tales of Hoffmann*, Rosina in the *Barber of Seville*, Pamina in the *Magic Flute* and Zerlina in *Don Giovanni*.

Traditionally, it has been more difficult for the black male than it has been for the black female to break into grand opera. Lawrence Winters was unable to make a living in opera in the United States and, therefore, went to perform in Europe. Although he sang with the New York City Center Opera, he was never engaged at the Metropolitan. The last time he was in New York he told his friend Andrew Frierson: "I would love to come home, but I just can't make a living here."

George Shirley was the first black male singer to blossom into a major artist at the Metropolitan. He made his debut when he replaced tenor Charles Anthony, who became ill before the second performance of the Met's 1961-62 season. He sang the role of Ferrando in Mozart's *Cosi Fan Tutte*.

In November of the same season he appeared in the lead role of Lieutenant Pinkerton in *Madama Butterfly*, in what was orginally scheduled as his debut, and once again the audience and critics were delighted.

Mr. Shirley is one of the most sought-after tenors on both sides of the Atlantic. He was the second black male singer to join the Metropolitan Opera roster in a solo capacity. "For blacks this wedding of music and drama is sort of the perfect outlet for what they had to say culturally," said George.

George was born in Indianapolis, Indiana, and was reared in Detroit, Michigan. Entirely American trained, he holds a Bachelor of Science degree in Music Education from Detroit's Wayne State University. Like William Warfield and Leontyne Price, he too had originally planned to become a teacher. While in the Army stationed at Fort Myers, Virginia, he met a vocal teacher who changed the course of his career.

Mr. Shirley won first prize in the Metropolitan Opera auditions in 1961 and has also been the recipient of a

National Arts Club Award, the Concorso di Vercelli in Italy and is an American Auditions winner.

Among the other roles in which Mr. Shirley has appeared at the Metropolitan are *The Magic Flute, Simon Boccanegra, La Traviata, The Barber of Seville, Falstaff, Elisir d'Amore* and *Lucia di Lammermoor*. He has made outstanding debuts at the Teatro Colon in Buenos Aires, Glyndebourne, Tanglewood, Hollywood Bowl, Covent Garden and with the Scottish National Opera.

Martina Arroyo has become one of the leading sopranos of the Metropolitan Opera. She is a top box-office attraction on both sides of the Atlantic Ocean and is one of America's busiest artists.

When cast at the Metropolitan in the role of Elsa in Wagner's *Lohengrin,* she became the first black woman to sing that part. During the same season she performed in eleven capital cities singing Amelia in Verdi's *Un Ballo in Maschera,* as well as debuts as Aïda at Covent Garden and at Buenos Aires' Teatro Colon.

A native New Yorker, Martina sang in school glee clubs and church choirs. It wasn't until she was in the Hunter High School that her extraordinary voice attracted attention. After graduating from Hunter College in three years, she worked as a grade school teacher and a social worker for a short time.

She was thrust into the music world in 1958 when she made her first appearance at Carnegie Hall in the American premiere of Pizetti's opera *Murder in the Cathedral.* That same year she won the Metropolitan Opera Auditions of the Air and made her Metropolitan debut as the offstage Celestial Voice in Verdi's *Don Carlo*. A guest contract brought Miss Arroyo more minor roles at the Met. Soon thereafter, the Vienna State Opera and the Deutsche Opera Berlin and other European opera houses offered major roles to the young artist.

Miss Arroyo's major break at the Metropolitan came in February, 1965, when she substituted for the ailing Birgit

Nilsson in the title role of *Aïda*. Her performance won phenomenal acclaim, and she was immediately offered a contract to sing such roles as Leonora in *Il Trovatore*, Elizabeth in *Don Carlo* and the title roles of *Aïda* and *Madama Butterfly*. When she sang her first *Madama Butterfly* the New York Times wrote: "Miss Arroyo sings magnificently. Hers was an illustrious interpretation, for Miss Arroyo has both the voice and the acting ability to make the part seem real and human . . ."

"Forever and ever people are coming up to me and saying, 'Miss Price, may I have your autograph?'" said Martina. Martina used to explain that she was not Leontyne. One lady was really insistent and said, "Oh, yes you are."

"Now I guess I am Leontyne Price," said Martina. "So now I will forget about what people think.

"I'm waiting for somebody to go up to you and say: 'Miss Arroyo, may I have your autograph?'" Martina once told Leontyne. Lee just laughed and said, "I'd just sign it."

One day Martina went to Louis Melancon's office, the famous photographer of opera singers. She wanted to select one of her own pictures. She saw a very striking one of herself onstage that was quite a distance away.

"There's one," she said excitedly.

"No, that's Lee—you big idiot," retorted Mr. Melancon.

While in Vienna, Martina went to a performance of *Il Trovatore* casting Leontyne Price and James McCracken. During the intermission a lady approached Martina and said: "Miss Price, may I have your autograph?"

"I'm not Miss Price. She's singing," responded Miss Arroyo.

"Oh yes, incognito," she said.

"Madame, my name is Anderson," Martina said and left abruptly.

Martina Arroyo is a frequent guest at Europe's great opera houses which include Vienna, Berlin, Stuttgart, Frankfurt and Geneva. She is also in demand in concert halls all over the Continent. In addition, she is a regular participant in the principal music festivals in the United States as well as abroad.

Grace Bumbry became an international celebrity when she sang the role of Venus in Wagner's *Tannhaeuser* at the famous Bayreuth Wagner Festival—the first black woman ever to do so. German "purists' objected to the appearance of an American woman of color in the tradionally blonde role, but she went on nevertheless and scored a tremendous success, taking innumerable curtain calls.

Hearing of her fame in Europe, Mrs. John F. Kennedy invited her to sing at a formal dinner she was giving for Washington officialdom. Thus, in a literal sense, Grace's formal American debut was made at the White House on February 20, 1962.

Born in Saint Louis, Missouri, Miss Bumbry grew up in a religious and musical household. She was the only daughter in the family, and she emulated her parents and her brothers by singing in a Methodist Church choir by the time she was eleven. Her vocal quality attracted the attention of the community and she entered several local competitions successfully. When she was sixteen, she had won several local competitions successfully. When she was seventeen a local radio station, KMOX, arranged for her to appear on Arthur Godfrey's Talent Scouts. She won first prize singing *"O don fatale"* from Verdi's *Don Carlo*.

A great many changes developed in the young mezzo-soprano's life after that occasion. She won scholarships which enabled her to study at Boston University and later at Northwestern University. It also brought her to the attention of the noted impresario, Sol Hurok. Profiting by Mr. Hurok's advice, Grace devoted her time to assiduous study. She specifically placed emphasis on singing technique, languages and acting, in addition to straight academic training.

In Europe, Miss Bumbry gave concerts in London and Paris. Her name became a household word among music lovers after her appearance at the Paris Opera where she appeared as Amneris in *Aïda* and starred in the title role of *Carmen.*

Although she resides in Germany, she does not like to sing opera in that country. She prefers to sing *lieder* and has quite a following in some of the major cities in Europe where she appears.

On October 7, 1965, Miss Bumbry made her debut at the Metropolitan Opera, singing the role of Princess Eboli in *Don Carlo.* After her sensational success, Alan Rich wrote in *The New York Herald Tribune* the followng day: "A beautiful tall striding woman with innate dramatic flair, Miss Bumbry filled Verdi's musical lines with creative fire . . . an exciting, magnetic, dynamic singer!"

Leontyne Price was out of town on tour when Grace made her triumphant debut. However, she had Hubert Dilworth send Miss Bumbry a big bottle of champagne. Grace was most impressed and delighted because she didn't know that Leontyne had even thought that much about her debut. "It was heartwarming to receive such a thing as that from a great artist like Leontyne. It was really wonderful," said Grace with tears in her eyes.

During the 1967-68 season, Miss Bumbry brought her portrayal of Carmen to the stage of the new Metropolitan Opera House. She had already sung the part of the fiery gypsy at the Salzburg Festival on July 27, 1966 in a performance under Herbert von Karajan. *The New York Times* reported that the performance was a rousing success and that Miss Bumbry received "thunderous applause for her singing and for her unconventionally sexy Carmen."

Felicia Weathers made her debut at the Metropolitan Opera House as Lisa in Tchaikowsky's stormy *Queen of Spades* in 1965. The twenty-seven-year-old soprano with a big, dramatic voice, had won the Metropolitan Opera auditions in 1957. Hailing from Saint Louis, Missouri, she was already a veteran singer with five distinguished years of experience on the Continent. Her repertoire had already grown to approximately sixty-three leading roles in five languages.

She had sung in at least forty opera houses of Europe. Her greatest roles are in the Italian repertoire. However, her interpretation of "Salome" aroused electrifying excitement among European operagoers. Mr. Bing wanted to engage her at the Met as soon as his attention was focused on her Elisabeth in *Don Carlo*.

Miss Weathers put aside medical studies at Washington University in Saint Louis to pursue a career in music, which had been her preferred area of concentration since early childhood. She later won a scholarship to Indiana University, where she continued voice studies under the aegis of two former Metropolitan performers, soprano Dorothee Manski and tenor Charles Kullman.

Shortly after her graduation, Felicia entered the international competition for young singers in Sofia, Bulgaria. For the audition, she selected the taxing Vision Scene from Menotti's *Saint of Bleecker Street*. The stunned audience broke the strict rule of forbidding applause. Awarded a Laureate, the then novice singer toured Bulgaria and then performed in Kiel, Germany, where in 1961 she first sang the title role of *Salome*. This engagement was instrumental in her being invited to sing the same role at the Munich Opera. Shortly afterwards, she was heard at Salzburg by Herbert von Karajan, who immediately engaged her with the Vienna Staatsoper.

It didn't take long for Felicia Weathers' European success to spread throughout the music world in the United States. Rudolf Bing invited her to Milan to sing in a private audition. It was this music session that led to a coveted contract with the Metropolian Opera Company.

The German critic, Horst Koegler, commented on her role of Elisabeth de Valois in the new production of *Don Carlo* in Cologne. Writing in the British magazine *Opera*, he noted that her interpretation of the part was "beautifully controlled and sensitively shaped."

Another editor of *Opera* was stunned by one of her performances. When he heard her for the first time he wrote: "*Madama Butterfly* was notable for Felicia Weathers' exquisite performance of the title role. This was one of the most fragile and convincing Cio-Cio-Sans I have ever seen or heard. The voice, anything but fragile, was used with infinite taste, and her impersonation was most touching."

Miss Weathers, like most of Metropolitan's renowned singers, joined the roster of the Chicago Lyric Opera. In her performance she sang the role of Renata in *The Flaming Angel*. Writing for *Opera News*, one critic wrote, "Through (the opera's) macabre landscape, Felicia Weathers was blown like a small, demented leaf. Her voice was large, dramatic and undaunted by Prokofiev's formidable chromatics and heavy orchestration." Her striking success opened the door for her to be immediately signed by the company to sing the role of Salome during the 1967 season.

That same year the soprano appeared at the Lincoln Center Festival with the touring Hamburg State Opera in Gunther Schuller's new opera, *The Visitation*. She sang the role of Teena, which she had created at the opera's world premiere in October, 1966.

The unique *bel canto* of Reri Grist has placed her in the forefront of the operatic world. She made a highly successful Metropolitan Opera debut on February 26, 1966, as Rosina in *The Barber of Seville*. "She is bewitching on stage—pert, beautiful, a wonderful ingénue. She is a most attractive singer who comes over the footlights in strong fashion," commented Harold Schonberg in *The New York Times*.

Born in New York City, Reri began early to acquire the wit and perception that were to distinguish her later. In 1946, while still a child, she made her acting debut on the Broadway stage in *Jeb*. She rapidly grew into more substantial roles in musical comedy. She appeared on Broadway as Cindy Lou in *Carmen Jones* and as Phyllis in *Shinbone*

Alley. One of her most notable parts was as Consuela in *West Side Story*. While she was doing minor parts in the theatre and singing to small audiences in New York, Reri attended the High School of Music and Art. She later earned a Bachelor of Arts Degree in Music in 1954 at Queens College in her native city.

Reri Grist is probably the only artist to "graduate" from musical comedy to the opera house and the concert hall. After she sang with the New York Philharmonic under the baton of Leonard Bernstein, there were no doubts about what route she would travel thereafter.

When Miss Grist decided to devote herself exclusively to grand opera and the concert field, she travelled to Santa Fe, New Mexico in 1959 to make her operatic debut in *The Abduction from the Seraglio* and *Die Fledermaus*.

Reri began her association with the Zurich Opera in 1960 making her debut as Zerbinetta in *Ariadne auf Naxos*. Her European reputation became wide and varied, and her musical gifts are equally respected in her native land. She made her debut at the Glyndebourne Festival in Sussex, England, in 1962 performing sixteen times as Despina in *Cosi Fan Tutte* and four times as Zerbinetta in *Ariadne auf Naxos*. That same year she sang the role of Queen of Shemakhan in *Le Coq d'Or* at Covent Garden. "America has given us an alluring queen with high soprano tones like small but dazzling diamonds, and a stage personality of equal brilliance," was a comment in the *London Times*.

She sang at La Scala, the Vienna Staatsoper and in San Francisco in 1963. In 1964 she performed at Salzburg and with the Chicago Lyric Opera in 1965.

Her repertoire continues to expand. It includes the role of Oscar in *Un Ballo in Maschera*, Sophia in *Der Rosenkavalier*, Norina in *Don Pasquale* and Susanna in *The Marriage of Figaro*. She has also performed the part of Lakmé.

Reri Grist joined the cast with Leontyne Price one season with the San Francisco Opera Company singing the role of

Oscar in *Un Ballo in Maschera*. After a magnificent performance Arthur Bloomfield wrote in the *San Francisco Examiner* on November 15, 1967: "The unimpeachable elements were the Amelia of Miss Price, the Oscar of Reri Grist and the conducting of Mario Bernardi . . . as for Miss Grist, *she's the world's champion Oscar*—crisp in voice, and just boyishly bumptious enough in action."

Another comment about the opera appeared in the *San Francisco Examiner* by Alexander Fried on November 20, 1967: "As Oscar (the Colonial Boston governor's boy page) Miss Grist was a perfect enchantment, in both her sparkling coloratura voice and her radiance of affection and fun."

Shirley Verrett, a brilliant mezzo-soprano, sang the title role of *Carmen* for her debut at the Metropolitan Opera House on Saturday evening, September 21, 1968. "Her mezzo voice has excitement built into it," wrote Miles Kastendieck. Bizet's masterpiece was far from new to Miss Verrett. She had successfully sung it abroad as well as in the United States.

Overtures had been made in 1961 for Miss Verrett to appear at the Met in other roles. However, she had her sights set on making her debut in the demanding and challenging role of Carmen. Shirley continued to study the role and she appeared in performances all over the United States, Canada, and the Soviet Union.

The critics as well as Miss Verrett awaited her debut night in her preferred role. Alan Rich of *New York Magazine* said: "The Carmen was and it's about time, Shirley Verrett, and she is superb." Writing of her interpretation of the role *Time* Magazine said: "Verrett's gypsy go-go girl was proud, alluring, panther-like, intelligent, and vocally velvet. Right at the start, in the opening Habanera, she rejected the tradition that makes Carmen a menacing *femme fatale*."

Born in New Orleans, Louisiana, and reared in Los Angeles, California, the stunning Miss Verrett was "discovered" during an appearance on the Arthur Godfrey talent show when she sang the aria "My Heart at Thy

Sweet Voice" from *Samson and Delilah*. After hearing the broadcast, Madame Marian Freschl, the renowned voice teacher, offered to take the young singer as a pupil and arranged for a scholarship with the Juilliard School of Music where Miss Verrett was graduated.

During her days at Juilliard, Miss Verrett entered every contest she could. Among her honors are the top vocal prize of the National Federation of Music Clubs, the Martha Baird Rockefeller Fund to Music, the John Charles Thomas Scholarship, the Ford Foundation Fellowship and the John Jay Whitney Foundation Award.

Miss Verrett made her formal New York debut with a recital in Philharmonic Hall in November, 1963. Since then her career in opera, concert and recital has continued to move rapidly. She has sung at Spoleto, at Montreal's Place des Arts, with the New York City Opera and the Pittsburgh Opera and with many leading American and European conductors and orchestras. Early in 1963 she made international headlines. She became the first black singer to appear in *Carmen* in Moscow's Bolshoi Theatre. In May, 1966, she made her Covent Garden debut as Ulrica in *Un Ballo in Maschera*, and in January 1967 participated in performances of the Verdi *Requiem* at La Scala, conducted by Herbert von Karajan.

On January 9, 1970, Shirley Verrett made a resounding debut in Milan, Italy, singing the female leading role in Saint-Saens' *Samson and Delilah*. Franco Abbiati, music critic of *Corriere della Sera*, described her instrument as the "voice of velvet." He called her "a proud enchantress" and "a Delilah who gushes sensuality with every note."

Miss Verrett was very surprised and pleased by the reaction of the audience to her first appearance in an opera role in Milan.

"The way the people screamed and yelled was astonishing," she said. "I was very impressed with the Milanese because I had heard they were usually quite cool."

APPENDIX A

LEONTYNE PRICE—SOPRANO

Principal Events

Born in Laurel, Mississippi—February 10—Daughter: James A. and Katherine Price. B.A. Central State University, Wilberforce, Ohio. Julliard School of Music.

1952 — Paris Debut—International Arts Festival—Virgil Thomson's *Four Saints in Three Acts.*

1953 — Debut as Bess in *Porgy and Bess.* Toured, Vienna, Berlin, Paris (auspices 20th Century Music Conference in Rome.)

1954 — Debut Recital Town Hall, New York. Samuel Barber at piano for *Hermit Songs.* Boston Symphony (Munch) debut. Philadelphia Orchestra (Ormandy) debut.

1955 — Debut NBC Opera Company—TV, title role *Tosca.* Debut Hollywood Bowl.

1956 — Debut American Opera Society as Cleopatra in Handel's *Julius Caesar.*
Debut San Francisco Symphony. Tour of India (auspices U.S. State Department) and Australia.

1957 — Debut San Francisco Opera—U.S. premiere of Poulenc's *Dialogues of the Carmelites.* Also U.S. debut as *Aïda.* Tour of Australia.

1958 — Debut Vienna Staatsoper (von Karajan). Debut Covent Garden (Kubelik). Debut Verona Arena (Serafin). Debut New York Philharmonic (Bern-

1960 — DON GIOVANNI. *Donna Anna.* NBC-TV Opera Company.
1961 — GIRL OF THE GOLDEN WEST. Mimi. Metropolitan Opera.
stein). Tour of Yugoslavia. Brussels' World's Fair (recitals).
1959 — Debut Salzburg Festival. Debut BBC—London—Orchestral (Peter Herman Adler). Recital (Gerald Moore).
Debut Chicago Lyric Opera.
Debut Vienna
Philharmonic (von Karajan).
1960 — Debut La Scala Opera. Debut Berlin Festival.
1961- Debut Metropolitan Opera, January 27, 1961—
1962   *Il Trovatore.*
Opening Night, Metropolitan Opera, October 23, 1961—*Girl of the Golden West.* Debut Lucerne Festival. Debut tour with Metropolitan Opera.
1963 — Debut Chicago Symphony Orchestra (Reiner). Represented Music World at *Time Magazine* 40th Anniversary Dinner.
1964 — Debut Soviet Union. Debut Berlin Opera.
1966 — Debut Teatro dell'Opera—Rome.
1968 — Debut Paris Opera.
1969 — Debut—Teatro Colon.
Opening Night, Met Opera.
Opening Concert, New Juilliard School at Lincoln Center, Alice Tully Hall.
1970 — Debut Hamburg Opera.

APPENDIX B

LEONTYNE PRICE

Opera Debuts

1952 — FALSTAFF. *Mistress Ford.* Juilliard School of Music.
1952 — FOUR SAINTS IN THREE ACTS. *Saint Cecelia.* International Arts Festival (New York and Paris).
1953 — PORGY AND BESS. *Female Title Role.* United States State Department.
1955 — TOSCA. *Title Role.* NBC-TV Opera Company.
1956 — THE MAGIC FLUTE. *Pamina.* NBC-TV Opera Company.
1956 — JULIUS CAESAR (Handel). *Cleopatra.* American Opera Society, New York.
1957 — DIALOGUES OF THE CARMELITES. *New Prioress.* San Francisco Opera.
1957 — AIDA. *Title Role.* San Francisco Opera.
1958 — IL TROVATORE. *Leonora.* San Francisco Opera.
1958 — THE WISE MAIDEN. *Title Role.* San Francisco Opera.
1958 — CORONATION OF POPPEA (Monteverdi). American Opera Society, New York.
1959 — DON GIOVANNI. *Donna Elvira.* San Francisco Opera.
1959 — THAIS. *Title Role.* Lyric Opera of Chicago.
1959 — TURANDOT. *Liu.* Lyric Opera of Chicago.
1960 — MADAMA BUTTERFLY, *Cio-Cio-San.* Vienna State Opera.

1962 — ERNANI. *Donna Elvira*. Metropolitan Opera.
1963 — EUGENE ONEGIN. *Tatiana*, Metropolitan Opera.
1963 — CARMEN. *Title Role*. Recorded with von Karajan, Corelli, Merril, Freni.
1963 — LA FORZA DEL DESTINO. *Leonora*. San Francisco Opera.
1964 — COSI FAN TUTTE. *Fiordiligi*. Metropolitan Opera.
1965 — UN BALLO IN MASCHERA. *Amelia*. San Francisco Opera.
1966 —ANTONY AND CLEOPATRA. *Cleopatra*. Metropolitan Opera.
1971 -- IL TABARRO. *Giorgetta*. San Francisco Opera.

APPENDIX C

LEONTYNE PRICE

Discography

RCA

Beethoven	Symphony No. 9
Bizet	*Carmen*
da Falla	*El Amor Brujo*
Berlioz	*Les Nuits d'Été*
Faure, Puccini, Strauss, Wolf	Songs
Gershwin	*Porgy and Bess*
Mozart	*Cosi Fan Tutte*
Puccini, Verdi	Operatic Arias
Puccini	*Madama Butterfly*
	Il Tabarro
Previn	Right As the Rain
Schumann	*Frauenliebe und Leben*
Strauss	*Salome/Aegyptische Helen*
Verdi	*Aïda*
	Ernani
	Il Trovatore
	La Forza del Destino
	Verdi Heroines
Spirituals (Collection)	"Swing Low, Sweet Chariot"
Spirituals (Collection)	"I Wish I Knew How It Would Feel to Be Free"
Favorite Hymns (Collection)	Leontyne Price My Favorite Hymns
Purcell to Barber	Leontyne Price Prima Donna I

215

Handel to Puccini	Leontyne Price Prima Donna II
Gluck to Poulenc	Leontyne Price Prima Donna III
Barber	Leontyne Price Two Scenes from *Antony and Cleopatra* "Knoxville: Summer of 1915"
Mozart	Leontyne Price Sings Mozart Operatic and Concert Arias

LONDON RECORDS

Mozart	*Don Giovanni*
Puccini	*Tosca*
Verdi	*Aïda*
	Requiem
Traditional	*A Christmas Offering*

COLUMBIA MASTERWORKS

Barber	"Hermit Songs"

APPENDIX D

LEONTYNE PRICE

Honors and Memberships

Presidential Medal of Freedom
Fellow, American Academy of Arts and Sciences
Honorary Doctorates: Dartmouth College; Howard University; Fordham University; Central State University; Rust College, 1969—New library named for Leontyne Price (Holly Springs, Miss.)
Trustee and Member of Board of Directors: International House
Member of Advisory Board: National Cultural Center, Washngton, D. C.
Spirit of Achievement Award: Albert Einstein College of Medicine
Honorary Vice-Chairman: U. S. National Committee of UNESCO
Voted Musician of the Year: *Musical America's* annual poll of music critics and editors
First artist to sing before integrated audiences (in Laurel, Mississippi)
Seventeen awards from National Academy of Recording Arts and Sciences (Grammy Awards)
Spingarn Medal—awarded by NAACP
Citation of Merit: New York Singing Teacher's Association
Time Magazine Cover Story
Order of Merit: Republic of Italy
Premiered role of Cleopatra in Samuel Barber's new opera

Antony and Cleopatra, opening night of new Metropolitan Opera House at Lincoln Center, 1966
Schwann Catalog—Award 1968
Billboard #1 in the Nation Award 1968
First Community Relations Award, Moore College of Art, 1970
Harper's Bazaar—"American Woman of Accomplishment" Award 1968 and 1971
Ladies' Home Journal—1971 "One of America's Most Important Women" Award
Vice-President: Whitney M. Young, Jr. Memorial Foundation, 1971

978-0-595-41699-8
0-595-41699-3